MULLIGAN'S
BAR GUIDE

APR - - 2012

MULLIGAN'S BAR GUIDE

to mixing, serving and otherwise consuming

COCKTAILS
LIQUEURS
&
SHOOTERS

Compiled & Lovingly Edited by

SHAWN M. MULLIGAN

25TH ANNIVERSARY EDITION

Collins

SPECIAL THANKS

Gertrude Mulligan, for all your support; Big Up to Debbonaire J. Reid for your support
and assistance; Bonnie Harris for starting things; Debbie Ruptash; Paul Plante;
Jacquie Ellicott; the Moumos family; Roy Nicol; Nicole Langlois;
Carolyn Black; and, finally, all those bartenders who let me try
their new creations during *RESEARCH* for this
new edition. Many thanks, and save
me a seat at the wood.

Mulligan's Bar Guide
© 1988, 2000, 2011 by Shawn Mulligan. All rights reserved.

Published by Collins, an imprint of HarperCollins Publishers Ltd.

First published by HarperCollins: 1989
This trade paperback edition: 2011

HarperCollins books may be purchased for educational, business, or sales promotional
use through our Special Markets Department.

HarperCollins Publishers Ltd
2 Bloor Street East, 20th Floor
Toronto, Ontario, Canada
M4W 1A8

www.harpercollins.ca

Library and Archives Canada Cataloguing in Publication
Mulligan, Shawn M.
Mulligan's bar guide / Shawn M. Mulligan.

ISBN 978-1-4434-0855-4

1. Cocktails. I. Title.

TX951.M85 2011   641.8´74   C2011-903681-9

Printed and bound in Canada
WEB 9 8 7 6 5 4 3 2 1

CONTENTS

If you don't see
what you're looking for, you've
come to the right place.
Optometrist's sign

TOASTS

A glass in the hand's worth
Two on the shelf—
Tipple it down and refresh
Yourself!
English

If I drink too much of your liquor,
And should be foolish enough to get tight,
Would you be a perfect gentleman,
And see that I get home all right?
Anonymous

May you have warm words on a cold evening,
A full moon on a dark night,
And the road downhill all the way to your door.
Irish

May you have food and raiment,
A soft pillow for your head,
May you be forty years in heaven,
Before the devil knows you're dead!
Irish

Dance as if no one were watching,
Sing as if no one were listening,
And live every day as if it were your last.
Irish

May you never lie, steal, cheat or drink.
But if you must lie, lie in each other's arms.
If you must steal, steal kisses.
If you must cheat, cheat death.
And if you must drink, drink with us, your friends.
Irish

May your health be like the capital of Ireland—
Always Dublin!
Irish

An Irishman is never drunk as long as
He can hold onto one blade of grass and not
Fall off the face of the earth.
Irish

Life, alas,
Is very drear.
Up with the glass,
Down with the beer!
Louis Untermeyer

May misfortune follow you the rest of your life,
But never catch up.
Irish

A toast to your coffin:
May it be made of 100-year-old oak.
And may we plant the tree together, tomorrow.
Irish

May the Irish hills caress you.
May her lakes and rivers bless you.
May the luck of the Irish enfold you.
May the blessings of Saint Patrick behold you.
Irish

May the leprechauns be near you,
To spread luck along your way,
And may all the Irish angels,
Smile upon you St. Patrick's Day.
Irish

May your heart be warm and happy
With the lilt of Irish laughter
Every day in every way
And forever and ever after.
Irish

Who is a friend but someone to toast,
Someone to give, someone to roast.
My friends are the best friends
Loyal, willing and able.
Now let's get to drinking!
Glasses off the table!
Irish

May you live to be a hundred years,
With one extra year to repent!
May your neighbors respect you,
Trouble neglect you,
The angels protect you,
And heavens accept you.
Irish

In all this world, why I do think
There are four reasons why we drink:
Good friends,
Good wine,
Lest we be dry
And any other reason why.
Irish

Many happy returns of the day of your birth:
Many blessings to brighten your pathway on earth;
Many friendships to cheer and provoke you to mirth:
Many feastings and frolics to add to your girth.
Robert H. Lord

"A wet night maketh a dry morning,"
Quoth Hendyng, "Rede ye right;
And the cure most fair is the self-same hair
Of the dog that gave the bite."
Punderson

Four and twenty Yankees,
feeling very dry,
Went across the border
to get a drink of rye,
When the rye was opened,
the Yanks began to sing
God bless America,
But God save the King!
Toast from Canada during Prohibition

Here's a toast to all those that we love,
Here's a toast to all those that love us,
Here's a toast to all those that love them
that love those that love them that love those that love us.
Anonymous

A Tudor who tooted a flute
tried to tutor two tooters to toot.
Said the two to their tutor,
"Is it harder to toot
or to tutor two tooters to toot?"
Anonymous Tongue Twister

FOREIGN PHRASES

Can you imagine dipping a piece of scorched bread into your Guinness or cabernet to enhance its flavor? The British could, and in the Middle Ages they called this practice "toasting." Today, thankfully, a "toast" is a short cheer to precede a tipple among friends. Below is a collection of cheers from around the world, and I ask that you please put them to good use. Cheers!

WHEN IN	YOU WOULD SAY	AND MEAN
Australia	Cheers!	Well ... Cheers!
China	Gan bei!	Dry your cup!
Denmark	Skal!	Salute to you!
Finland	Kippis!	Cheers!
France	A votre santé!	To your health!
Germany	Prosit!	Cheers!
Great Britain	Cheers!	(They invented it!)
Greece	Stin ygia sou!	To your health!
Hawaii	Kamau!	Here's how!
Iceland	Skal!	Salute to you!
Ireland	Slainthe is saol agat!	Health and life to you!
Israel	L'chaim!	To life!
Italy	Cin-cin!	All good things for you!
Japan	Kanpai!	Dry cup!
Mexico	¡Salud!	Health!
Russia	Za vashe zdorovye!	To health!
Saudi Arabia	Hanian!	Congratulations!
Scotland	Slainte mhoiz!	Good health!
Spain	¡Salud!	To your health!
Turkey	Serefinize!	To your health!
Wales	Lechyd da!	God be with you!

Crossword #1

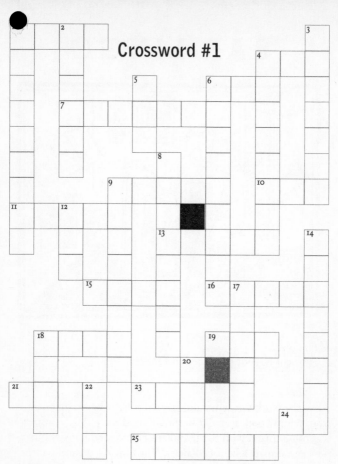

ACROSS

1. Cuba Libra mixer
4. top-fermented beer
6. juniper-flavored spirit
7. cordial
9. Russia's spirit
10. _ _ _ Maria
11. passion fruit liqueur
13. martini garnish
15. seltzer
16. intoxicating alcohol type
18. dry Champagne
19. Champagne & cassis
21. without ice
23. draft Guinness is one
24. fine cognac classification
25. pousse-cafés have them

DOWN

1. orange liqueur named for an island
2. Mexican coffee liqueur
3. agave distillate without the worm
4. clear absinthe substitute
5. sugar cane spirit
6. pomegranate syrup
8. Dutch "eggnog"
9. martinis need it
12. rocks
14. Italian herb-licorice liqueur
17. lemon peel garnish
18. Homer's beverage
20. 1 oz. shot
22. 20%?

solution p. 133

BAR LINGO

Abricotine
An apricot liqueur produced in France.

Absinthe
Absinthe is a bitter, emerald-green alcoholic beverage made from wormwood. Popular in the 19th and early 20th centuries, it was often mixed with sugar and aniseed to moderate its bitterness and impart a licorice flavor. When mixed, absinthe turns opaque white. Chronic absinthe drinkers began to suffer from symptoms of hyperactivity, addiction and hallucinations; consequently, most countries banned its use around 1900. Vincent van Gogh and Ernest Hemingway were absinthe drinkers. Sambuca, anisette and ouzo are modern replacements.
> See also
> *dmoz.org/Recreation/Food/Drink/Liquor/Absinthe*
> *www.sepulchritude.com/chapelperilous*

Advocaat (a.k.a. Advokaat)
Advocaat is a mixture of sweetened egg yolks and brandy. Its name is derived from the Dutch word for "lawyer," as it tends to make imbibers talkative. Eggnog is a good substitute.

Afrikoko
A chocolate-coconut-flavored liqueur from South Africa.

Akvavit
See **Aquavit**

Alcohol
Ethanol is the chemical name for the main intoxicating ingredient in liquors, liqueurs and wines. Since ancient times, ethanol has been produced by the fermentation of sugars, through the introduction of yeast. The chemical formula for ethanol is CH_3CH_2OH, and there are no substitutes.
See also
www.scifun.chem.wisc.edu/chemweek/PDF/ethanol.pdf

Alizé
A cognac-based liqueur flavored with natural passion fruit. Try it with Champagne!

Amaretto
An almond-flavored liqueur produced from apricot pits.

Amer Picon
A French, bitter orange liqueur containing cinchona bark, gentian, oranges and quinine.

Angostura Bitters
Dr. J.G.B. Siegert created Angostura bitters in 1824. The Siegert family of Trinidad holds its secret recipe, but this much is known: Angostura is a rum-based spirit with some, all or none of the following ingredients: angostura bark, bitter orange and lemon peel, calisaya bark, cardamom, carob, cinnamon bark, cloves, ginger and tonka beans. Some other bitters are Abbott's from Baltimore, Peychaud from New Orleans and orange from England. The latter are made from dried Seville orange peels.
See also *www.angostura.com*

Anisette
Anisette is a licorice-flavored distillation of mature anise and star seeds, which was originally used as a tonic and aphrodisiac.

Applejack
A brandy produced through the fermentation of apples rather than grapes. The finest applejack is the French calvados.

Aquavit
Scandinavian vodka infused with caraway and dill seeds, herbs and spices—literally, "water of life."

Armagnac
A fine French brandy, which like all brandies (except flavored) is made from distilled wines. Armagnac was produced 150 years before cognac, yet never reached the same status. The best (most expensive) Armagnacs have the words "Grand-Bas-Armagnac" or simply "Grand Bas" on their label.
    See also *www.charlesnealselections.com/armagnac.html*

Aurum
An Italian, brandy-based liqueur flavored with oranges and saffron.

Bahai
A Brazilian, coffee-flavored liqueur.

Baileys
Baileys Irish Cream is the marriage of fresh dairy cream and triple-distilled, Irish, pot-still whiskey. This much-loved liqueur was introduced in 1974, reaching near cult status during the shooter revolution of the 1980s. Be sure to visit its website.
    See also *www.baileys.com/*

B & B
A mixture of cognac and Bénédictine.

Beer
A "most tasty" beverage resulting from the fermentation of malted barley, corn and/or rye, yeast and water.

Bénédictine
The Bénédictine monks at Fécamp Abbey in France concocted their recipe in 1510. Bénédictine was banned after the French Revolution and didn't resurface until 1863, when monastery lawyers rediscovered the formula amongst old documents and resumed production with an updated version. Though the exact prescription remains secret, it is known to include juniper, myrrh, angelica, cloves, cardamom, cinnamon, vanilla, tea and honey. For those of you who are label-readers, the letters "D.O.M." stand for "Deo Optimo Maximo" or "Praise to God most good, most great."

Bitters
See **Angostura Bitters**

Borouvička
A Czechoslovakian, juniper-flavored brandy.

Bourbon
An American whiskey named for Bourbon County in Kentucky. New oak barrels are used for this highly regulated distillation of at least 51% corn. To earn its title, this whiskey must be aged for a minimum of two years.

Brandy
Wine is produced through the fermentation of grapes, yeast and water, and brandy is a distillate of wine. Brandy's unique color and flavor are derived from its contact with oak and impurities such as oils, acids, mineral salts and tannins. Flavored brandies are produced through the fermentation of various fruits.

Brandy Classifications
v.e.f.c. Very extra fine cognac.
v.e.o.x.f. Very especially old extra cognac.
v.o. Very old cognac.
v.s. Very superior cognac.
v.s.o. Very superior old cognac.
v.s.o.p. Very special old pale cognac.
v.s.p. Very special pale cognac.
x.o. Extra old cognac.

Brut
A term used to denote the driest champagnes.

Cachaça
A potent Brazilian, tequila/rum-like spirit distilled from fermented sugar cane juice.

Calvados
A high-quality French brandy, produced from the fermentation of small, bitter apples.

Campari
A very dry and bitter Italian aperitif with a strong quinine taste.
See also *www.campari.com*

Chambord
A black raspberry liqueur produced in France.

Chambraise
A French, strawberry-flavored liqueur.

Chartreuse
The La Grande Chartreuse monastery in France originally produced this very secret blend of over 140 herbs, plants and spices. Two varieties exist: the yellow is flavored with saffron and is sweeter and lighter, while the green is high in alcohol content and spicier.

See also *www.chartreuse.fr*

Cheri-Suisse
A cherry-chocolate-flavored, Swiss liqueur.

Cognac
A high-quality brandy produced in the Cognac region of western France.

See also **Brandy Classifications**

Cointreau
Named after its inventors, Adolphe and Édouard Cointreau, this popular liqueur is produced from a fermentation of sweet and bitter orange peels.

See also *www.cointreau.com*

Cordial
A synonym for liqueur.

"Crème de" Liqueurs
In this instance "crème" does not stand for "cream" but rather a smooth, intense, cream-like liqueur. The following list matches names to flavors.

Crème d'Ananas—pineapple
Crème de Banane—banana
Crème de Cacao—chocolate
Crème de Café—coffee
Crème de Cassis—black currant
Crème de Ciel—orange
Crème de Fraise—strawberry
Crème de Framboise—raspberry
Crème de Menthe—peppermint

Crème de Mocha—coffee
Crème de Noisette—hazelnut
Crème de Noyaux—almond
Crème de Poire—pear
Crème Yvette—violet

Cuarenta y Tres

A complex, brandy-based Spanish liqueur flavored with vanilla and herbs.

Curaçao

The peels of small, green Curaçao oranges flavor this bitter, Caribbean liqueur. Curaçao comes in several colors—clear, orange, red, green and blue—but all have the same flavor.

Demerara Rum

A strong, full-bodied rum that was originally produced in Guyana.

Distillation

Ethyl alcohol has a lower boiling point (or volatility) than water. Consequently, if these ingredients are heated above the volatility of ethyl alcohol but below that of water, the alcohol will release as steam. The production and collection of that steam, or concentrated alcohol, is called distillation.

See also **Fermentation**

Drambuie

A Scottish blend of Highland malt Scotch whiskey, herbs and heather honey. The Gaelic name means "the drink that satisfies."

Dubonnet

A dry French aperitif that combines red and white wines with a concentration of red grape juice and spirits, sharpened by the addition of quinine.

Falernum

A sweet Caribbean syrup flavored with ginger, almonds, fruits, herbs and spices.

Fermentation

When sugar, yeast, water and heat are combined, ethyl alcohol and carbon dioxide are produced. The sugar often comes from either fruit or grain. Wine was one of the first alcoholic beverages to be produced because grape juice contains sugar and water, while grape skins hold yeast. Of course, the production of 21st century wine is considerably more complex, but the first wines literally made themselves.

See also **Distillation**

Frangelico
An Italian liqueur flavored with hazelnuts, berries and flowers.

Galliano
An Italian secret blend of over thirty herbs, roots, berries and flowers resulting in a spicy-sweet licorice flavor. The battle depicted on the label is that of the liqueur's namesake, Major Giuseppe Galliano.

Gin
Gin is a grain-distilled spirit flavored primarily with juniper berries. The minor ingredient list is long and includes coriander, fennel, anise, caraway, licorice, almonds, barks and lemon and orange peels.

See also **Distillation**, **Fermentation**

Glayva
A Scottish liqueur which is quite similar to Drambuie, in flavor and ingredients.

Goldwasser
A four-century-old liqueur combining citrus and spice flavors, known for its suspension of 22k gold flakes.

Grand Marnier
A popular French liqueur that blends fine cognac, spices and Caribbean oranges.

See also *www.grand-marnier.com*

Grappa
A strong Italian brandy distilled from the leftovers of wine production (i.e., grape skins, seeds and stalks).

Grenadine
A sweet, non-alcoholic syrup made from pomegranate juice. To make your own combine

1 cup water

1–2 pomegranates (peeled)
frozen strawberries or raspberries
1 cup sugar

Gently boil water with fruit for 30 minutes, then strain through cheesecloth until clear. Return to heat, add sugar and stir for 5 minutes, until sugar has dissolved. Cool, and it's ready to use.

Heineken
The Dutch beer that my friend Kevin drinks.

Hypnotiq
A blend of exotic juices, vodka and a touch of Cognac.

Ice
Profit.

Irish Mist
An Irish liqueur blending several herbs, heather honey and Irish whiskey.

Jägermeister
The name Jägermeister translates to "hunt master" in German. This liqueur was introduced in Germany over a century ago. Jägermeister consists of fifty-six fruits, spices and herbs, producing a bitter-sweet liqueur. While this liqueur is usually downed with a wince, I recommend sipping it alongside a chilled glass of strong beer, as it was intended.
  See also *www.jagermeister.com*

Kahlúa
A Mexican, brandy-based liqueur made from cocoa, coffee and vanilla beans.
  See also *www.kahlua.com*

Kirsch (a.k.a. Kirschwasser)
A dry, clear liqueur made from the kernels of maraschino cherries.

Kummel
A Dutch herb liqueur flavored with anise, caraway, cumin and coriander seeds.

Licor 43
See **Cuarenta y Tres**

Mescal (a.k.a. Mezcal)
See **Tequila**

Metaxa
A fiery Greek brandy made from muscat grapes.

Orgeat
A non-alcoholic almond syrup.

Ouzo
A Greek, licorice-flavored liqueur that turns milky when mixed with ice.
See also **Absinthe, Anisette and Sambuca**

Parfait Amour
A French, brandy-based liqueur, flavored with lemons, oranges and herbs. *Parfait Amour* means "perfect love."

Peychaud's Bitters
A pungent, licorice-flavored bitter produced in Louisiana.
See also **Angostura Bitters**

Pimm's Cup
An English line of fruit-based cocktails. Pimm's No. 1 has a gin base; No. 2, a whiskey base; No. 3, a rum base and No. 4, a brandy base.

Pousse-Café
A style of layered drink prepared by gently adding each ingredient from densest to least dense in order to create coloured stripes when the drink is viewed from the side. The drink is made primarily as a delight for the eye. It is sipped sometimes through a silver straw, one liqueur at a time. The drink must be created and handled carefully or the layers will mix together in a brown sludge.

Reggae
The national music of Jamaica, offering a relaxed style, complex rhythms and intense lyrics. Reggae is best enjoyed with a bottle of Guinness or Heineken; however, wine is also a great accompaniment. If you're new to this genre, I recommend Buju

Banton, Beenie Man, Beres Hammond and, of course, the great Bob Marley. What does this have to do with bartending? If you're enjoying libations, you're probably listening to music (unless a hockey game is on!). I recommend reggae.

Rock and Rye
An alcoholic fruit beverage consisting of rock candy, rye whiskey and fruit slices.
    See also **Rye Whiskey**

Rum
Rum is distilled from fermented sugar cane juice or molasses. Its color range, from white to dark, is the result of fermentation and distillation processes and the addition of caramel.
    See also **Distillation, Fermentation**

Rye Whiskey
Rye is distilled from a grain mash containing a minimum of 51% rye, a hardy grass containing a dark grain.
    See also **Distillation, Fermentation**

Sabra
An Israeli liqueur flavored with Jaffa oranges and chocolate.

Sake
A Japanese wine produced from the fermentation of rice rather than grapes.
    See also **Distillation, Fermentation**

Sambuca
A popular Italian licorice liqueur, often served flaming with three coffee beans floating on top.
    See also *www.luxardo.it*

Scotch
Scotch is produced from the fermentation of malted barley, which has been dried over peat fires to impart a smoky flavor. Scotch is made only in Scotland.
    See also **Distillation, Fermentation**

Sloe Gin
Sloe gin is a sweet liqueur made by infusing sloe berries of the blackthorn plum into gin.

Southern Comfort
A peach-flavored liqueur produced in the United States.
See also *www.southerncomfort.com*

Stars
Stars indicate the number of years old that a brandy is.

Strega
An Italian liqueur that is made with over seventy unique herbs, whose name means "witch."

Tequila
Bottles of tequila do not contain worms; however, bottles of tequila's relative, mescal, often do. By Mexican law, tequila must derive a minimum of 51% of its sugars from the blue agave plant, while mescal can be made from five different varieties of agave. Additionally, tequila is distilled at least twice, producing a smoother product, while mescal is often single-distilled.
See also **Distillation, Fermentation**

Tia Maria
A product of five-year-old Jamaican rum and Blue Mountain coffee beans.

Triple Sec
A clear, sweet liqueur flavored with Curaçao oranges.

Vodka
Vodka is a colorless, flavorless and odorless spirit produced through the fermentation and distillation of potatoes, wheat, corn or rye. Ingredients are secondary—the production of ethyl alcohol is primary. Since vodka is simply alcohol and water, without additives, it is hangover friendly.
See also **Distillation, Fermentation**

V.S.O.P., X.O., etc...
See **Brandy Classifications**

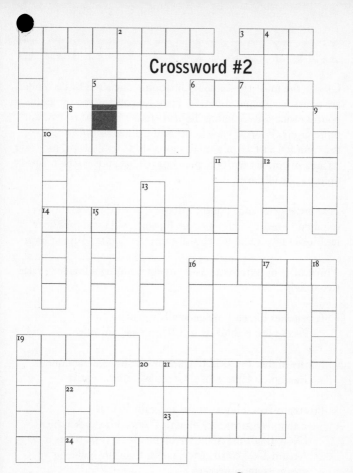

Crossword #2

ACROSS

1. French raspberry liqueur
3. Bazooka _ _ _
5. Rob _ _ _
6. "Cheers" bartender
10. absinthe replacement
11. _ _ _ _ _ 649
14. Cruise's character in *Cocktail*
16. Manhattan's garnish
19. Kramer's first name
20. beer with ginger ale
23. Planter's _ _ _ _ _
24. lager & lime cordial

DOWN

1. pousse- _ _ _ _

2. _ _ _ _ _ Cow
4. _ _ _ Fashioned
7. Greek licorice liqueur
8. crème _ _ banane
9. "love" in France
10. _ _ _ _ _ _ _ Amour
11. Monkey's _ _ _ _ _
12. bartender's bill
13. Fuzzy _ _ _ _ _
15. _ _ _ _ _ _ _ Slammer
16. "Cheers" waitress
17. _ _ _ _ _ Nail
18. agent of fermentation
19. _ _ _ _ _ White
21. beer's flavor comes from them
22. Champagne & cassis

solution p. 134

LAYERING GUIDE

Clearly the most eye-catching libations concocted by bartenders are pousse-cafés and shooters. They are constructed by skillfully pouring successively lighter liqueurs into a rainbow of two or more layers. Pouring each liqueur atop a maraschino cherry or the rounded surface of a small spoon slows its descent, increases its area of contact with the previous cordial and assists in developing a "clean" layer.

A knowledge of each liqueur's density, or relative weight, is required in order to know which liqueurs will form the "heavier," lower layers and which will form the "lighter," upper layers.

Three rules of thumb can assist in determining a liqueur's relative weight:

(1) sweeter liqueurs are generally heavier
Examples: Kahlúa, crème de banane, anisette

(2) the higher the alcohol content, the lighter the liqueur
Examples: Chartreuse, Grand Marnier, tequila

(3) cream-based liqueurs are generally lighter
Examples: advocaat, Baileys, Crème Grand Marnier
(Note that the "crème" in crème de menthe refers to a "cream-like" consistency, rather than the inclusion of cream as an ingredient.)

The chart on the facing page lists denser liqueurs first. For example, Parfait Amour (#12) layers below Frangelico (#32). If faced with the dilemma of layering two liqueurs which are not listed, follow this simple experiment to uncover the heaviest.

Let's call the respective liqueurs A and B. Now, pour a small amount of A into a shot glass and attempt to layer B atop it. One of three outcomes will result:

(1) B layers atop A, so A is heavier

(2) B flows through A, creating a layer beneath it, meaning B is heavier

(3) B and A merge, indicating they have similar densities

Get some "hands-on" experience with one of the pousse-café recipes listed in the "Shooters" section, or craft your own masterpiece.

	LIQUEUR	FLAVOR
1	Grenadine	Pomegranate / Berries
2	Chambord	Raspberry
3	Crème de Cassis	Black Currant
4	Dark Crème de Cacao	Chocolate
5	Kahlúa	Coffee
6	Café Royal	Coffee
7	Strawberry Liqueur	Strawberry
8	Peach Schnapps	Peach
9	Crème de Banane	Banana
10	Swiss Chocolate Almond	Chocolate Almond
11	Anisette	Licorice
12	Parfait Amour	Orange
13	Crème de Menthe	Mint
14	Liqueur d'Oro	Spiced
15	Chocolate Almond	Chocolate Almond
16	Melon	Melon
17	Tia Maria	Coffee / Rum
18	Cherry Brandy	Cherry
19	Apricot Brandy	Apricot
20	Advocaat	Cream / Egg
21	Sambuca (Black or White)	Licorice
22	Galliano	Licorice / Spice
23	Blue Curaçao	Orange
24	Amaretto	Almond
25	Triple Sec	Orange
26	Drambuie	Spice
27	Alizé	Passion Fruit
28	Bénédictine	Spice
29	Yellow Chartreuse	Spice
30	Campari	Bitter Herb
31	Peppermint Schnapps	Mint
32	Frangelico	Hazelnut
33	Spearmint Schnapps	Mint
34	Baileys Irish Cream	Vanilla / Whiskey
35	Crème Grand Marnier	Orange
36	Irish Mist	Mint
37	Cointreau	Orange

BARWARE CODE

Flute

Snifter

Pint glass

Highball

Wine

Shake

Rocks

Pony
(or Liqueur glass)

Strain

Cocktail

Mug

Build

Martini

Blender

Layer

COCKTAILS

Although the word "cocktail" first appeared in 1806, no one knows how or why it came about. The cocktail as we now know it was popularized during Prohibition when fruit, sugar and bitters were combined with foul-tasting semi-potables to render them palatable.

You won't, however, find a long, drawn-out list of unfamiliar drinks in this book, like "Flames over New Jersey" or "Duke of Marlborough"... and you won't have to smuggle any of the ingredients in from exotic vacation spots. What you will find is the most up-to-date collection of recipes anywhere.

Alabama Slammer
½ oz. Southern Comfort
½ oz. Amaretto
2 oz. lemon juice
*Shake ingredients with ice.
Strain into a martini glass.*

Alexander
1½ oz. brandy or gin
½ oz. white crème de cacao
2 oz. cream
garnish: grated nutmeg
*Shake ingredients with ice.
Strain into a martini glass.*

Alizé Sunrise
1 ½ oz. Alizé Gold
1 ½ oz. Alizé Red Passion
*Fill a martini glass with crushed
ice. Pour the two liqueurs down
opposite sides of the glass.*

Almond Colada
1 oz. Amaretto
1 /2 oz. Malibu rum
1 oz. coconut syrup
3 oz. cream
*Blend ingredients with ice. Pour
into a highball glass.*

Almond Joy Martini
1 oz. vodka
½ oz. Frangelico
½ oz. white crème de cacao
dash of coconut syrup
garnish: shredded coconut or
a Hershey's Kiss or two ;-) —
or both

*Shake ingredients with ice and
strain into a martini glass. You
must be all grown-up to enjoy
this booze-candy treat! No
minors allowed.*

Americano
1 oz. Rosso Cinzano
1 oz. Campari
soda water to fill
garnish: orange slice
*Build ingredients over ice into a
rocks glass.*

Appleberry Cocktail
1½ oz. vodka
½ oz. sour apple liqueur
1 oz. cranberry juice
2 oz. apple juice
1 oz. raspberry purée
garnish: apple slice and mint
sprig
*Shake ingredients with ice and
strain into a highball glass.*

Apple Jack
1 oz. Jack Daniel's
3 oz. apple juice
*Pour ingredients over ice into a
rocks glass.*

Appletini

2 oz. gin
1 oz. apple liqueur
2 oz. apple juice
1 oz. lime juice
Shake ingredients with ice and strain into a martini glass. Garnish with a lemon wedge.

Après Ski

½ oz. Kahlúa
½ oz. white crème de cacao
½ oz. peppermint schnapps
3 oz. cream
Blend ingredients thoroughly with ice. Pour into a cocktail glass.

Apricotini

1½ oz. apricot brandy
½ oz. gin
1 oz. orange juice
¼oz. lemon juice
Shake ingredients with ice and strain into a martini glass. Garnish with a piece of dried apricot, either on the rim, dropped in, or on the side.

Apricot Mojito

2 oz. dark rum
1 oz. apricot brandy
½ tsp. brown sugar
6 or 7 mint leaves
½ oz. lime juice
Muddle mint leaves and lime juice in a shaker filled with ice. Add remaining ingredients and shake firmly, then strain into a martini glass. Garnish with a mint sprig.

Bacardi Cocktail

2 oz. Bacardi rum
2 oz. lime juice
¼ oz. grenadine
garnish: lime wedge
To create this martini-style cocktail, shake ingredients with ice. Strain into a martini glass. This cocktail was invented during Prohibition by Jennings Cox, an American mining engineer. A popular choice in Cuban bars and nightclubs during that period, it remains popular today.

Bahama Mama

1 oz. dark rum
½ oz. coconut liqueur
½ oz. Kahlúa
½ oz. overproof rum
1 oz. lemon juice
2 oz. pineapple juice
Build ingredients into a highball glass over ice. Garnish with a cherry or a pineapple spear or both.

Banana Bliss

1½ oz. white rum
½ oz. crème de banane

1 oz. orange juice
2 oz. cream
Blend ingredients thoroughly with ice. Pour into a large cocktail glass.

Banana Boat

¹/₂ oz. vodka
¹/₂ oz. crème de banane
1 oz. orange juice
2 oz. cream
Blend ingredients thoroughly with ice and pour into a large cocktail glass.

Banana Daiquiri

1¹/₂ oz. white rum
¹/₂ oz. crème de banane
3 oz. lime juice
¹/₂ banana (optional but good!)
garnish: lime
Blend ingredients thoroughly with ice and pour into a large cocktail glass.

Banana Sandwich

1 oz. crème de banane
¹/₂ oz. white crème de cacao
2 oz. cream
Shake ingredients thoroughly with ice. Strain into a martini glass.

Bartender's Choice

1¹/₂ oz. whatever
1 oz. why not?
¹/₂ oz. nearest juice
¹/₄ oz. what he or she says
Shake ingredients with ice and strain into a martini glass. Garnish? You decide!

Bartender's Root Beer

1 oz. Kahlúa
¹/₂ oz. Galliano
3 oz. Coke
2 oz. soda water
garnish: cherry
Pour ingredients over ice into a highball glass.

Batida de Coco

2 oz. cachaça
3 oz. coconut milk
2 oz. condensed milk
simple syrup to taste
Shake ingredients firmly with ice and strain into a martini glass. A little taste of Brazil that's worth the ingredient search.

Batida de Fresa

2 oz. cachaça
¹/₂ oz. strawberry liqueur
2 oz. condensed milk
Shake firmly and strain into a martini glass. A note when ordering this Brazilian classic: "batida" is pronounced "BA-CHI-DA"; "cachaça" is pronounced "kak-SHAH-sa".

Beautiful

12 oz. Courvoisier
¹/₂ oz. Grand Marnier
garnish: orange slice
Pour ingredients into a snifter.

Bellini Classic

4 oz. Champagne
2 oz. peach purée
¹/₂–1 oz. simple syrup

Pour the peach purée into a chilled martini glass and top with Champagne. Garnish with a fresh peach slice, if possible. The Bellini was invented by Giuseppe Cipriani in 1948 at the famous Harry's Bar in Venice and is named after 17th-century Venetian painter Giovanni Bellini. A favorite of my friend Debbonaire.

Bellini II
1 oz. vodka
½ oz. peach schnapps
2–3 oz. Champagne
raspberries
Shake first two ingredients with ice and strain into a martini glass. Top with Champagne. Garnish with raspberries, preferably soaked in vanilla vodka until they double in size. The Bellini gives you the opportunity to experiment, so play around with unique garnishes and presentations. Bartenders don't simply mix cocktails—they create them.

Bermuda Cocktail
1 oz. gin
½ oz. apricot brandy
½ oz. curaçao
1 oz. lemon juice
dash of grenadine
Shake ingredients with ice and strain into a martini glass. Garnish with three twists— lemon, lime and orange.

Berry-Tini
1 oz. Kahlúa
1 oz. vanilla vodka
½ oz. raspberry liqueur
1 oz. cream
Shake ingredients with ice and strain into a martini glass.

Between the Sheets
¾ oz. white rum
¾ oz. brandy
½ oz. Cointreau
2 oz. lemon juice
Shake ingredients over ice. Strain into a martini glass.

Binary Martini
0b0100 parts vodka
0b0010 parts Parfait Amour
0b0001 part crème de banane
Shake ingredients firmly with ice, following the sequence 0101011010101011, using differential Manchester encoding, with amplitude of two arms' lengths, peak-to-peak.. Right rotate into a martini glass, discarding the rotated bit. Serve on a blank Blu-ray coaster. And remember—there are ten types of people in this world: those who know binary, and those who don't! Iterate.

Black and Tan
½ Guinness
½ pale ale (Bass if available)
Layer Guinness atop the ale. Experiment with several different ales until you find one that layers nicely. Quickly consume your mistakes.

Black Russian
1 oz. vodka
½ oz. Kahlúa
Pour ingredients over ice into a rocks glass.

Black Velvet
4 oz. chilled Champagne
8 oz. Guinness stout
Pour Champagne into a tall highball glass. Slowly add Guinness and stir gently.

The best audience is intelligent, well educated and a little drunk.
   Alben W. Barkley

Blarney Stone
1 oz. whiskey
½ oz. Pernod
½ oz. Chambord
dash of bitters
garnish: orange twist
Shake ingredients over ice. Strain into a martini glass.

Bloody Caesar
1 oz. vodka
5 oz. Clamato juice
Tabasco sauce
Worcestershire sauce
salt and pepper
Moisten the glass's rim with a lime wedge and coat it with celery salt. Pour vodka and Clamato over ice. Spice to taste. This very popular Canadian cocktail was invented in 1969 by Calgarian bartender Walter Chell. Popular garnishes are olives, asparagus tips, jalapeño peppers or prawns.

Bloody Mary
1 oz. vodka
5 oz. tomato juice
Tabasco sauce
Worcestershire sauce
salt and pepper
garnish: lemon wedge
Pour vodka and tomato juice over ice. Spice to taste.

Blue Angel
1½ oz. brandy
½ oz. Parfait Amour
2 oz. lemon juice
3 oz. cream
Shake ingredients over ice. Strain into a martini glass.

Blueberry Tea
1 oz. Amaretto
1 oz. Grand Marnier
garnish: orange wedge
tea on the side

Pour ingredients into a snifter.
Serve with a pot of hot tea on
the side.

Blue Hawaiian
1 oz. white rum
½ oz. blue curaçao
2 oz. pineapple juice
2 oz. orange juice
1 oz. coconut syrup
garnish: 1 slice pineapple
and/or cherry
Blend ingredients with ice and
pour into a large cocktail glass.

Blue Martini
1½ oz. gin
½ oz. blue curaçao
Shake ingredients over ice.
Strain into a martini glass.

Blue Meanie
1 oz. crème de banane
1 oz. blue curaçao
½ oz. lime juice
½ oz. orange juice
Shake ingredients with ice and
strain into a martini glass.

Blue Monday
1½ oz. vodka
½ oz. Parfait Amour
3 oz. 7UP
Pour ingredients over ice into a
tall highball glass.

Boomshackalacka
1 oz. currant vodka
½ oz. Chambord

½ oz. cherry brandy
½ oz. Malibu rum
2 oz. cranberry juice
Garnish: a lemon slice
Shake ingredients with ice and
strain into a martini glass.

Bramble
1½ oz. gin
1½ oz. lemon juice
½ oz. simple syrup
½ oz. blackberry liqueur
Shake first three ingredients with
ice and strain over crushed ice in
a rocks glass. Drizzle blackberry
liqueur into cocktail. Garnish
with lemon wedge, slice or twist.

Brandy Alexander
See *Alexander*

Brave Bull
1 oz. tequila
1 oz. Tia Maria
Pour ingredients over ice into a
rocks glass.

Brown Cow
1 oz. Kahlúa
3 oz. milk
Pour ingredients over ice into a
rocks glass.

Bull Shot
1 oz. vodka
3 oz. cold beef bouillon
Worcestershire sauce
Tabasco sauce
salt and pepper

Shake vodka and bouillon thoroughly with ice. Pour into a highball glass. Spice to taste.

Burnt Martini
2½ oz. gin
½ oz. premium Scotch
Some prefer the Scotch to be swirled around the martini glass, and then discarded before gin is poured in. Others shake both ingredients firmly with ice, then strain into a martini glass. Garnish with olives.

Buttery Ripple Martini
2 oz. butter ripple schnapps
1 oz. Baileys
1 oz. cream
Shake ingredients with ice and strain into a martini glass.

What's worth doing is worth doing for money.
Joseph Donohue

Caesar
See *Bloody Caesar*

Café Amaretto
1 oz. Amaretto
1 oz. Kahlúa
coffee
whipped cream
garnish: cherry
Moisten and sugar snifter's rim. Pour liqueurs and coffee. Top with whipped cream and a dash of Kahlúa.

Café Diablo
1 oz. brandy
½ oz. Grand Marnier
½ oz. sambuca
½ oz. Kahlúa
coffee
whipped cream
garnish: cherry
*See **Café Amaretto** for instructions.*

Café Supreme
1 oz. brandy
½ oz. triple sec
½ oz. Kahlúa
coffee
whipped cream
garnish: cherry
*See **Café Amaretto** for instructions.*

California Iced Tea
⅕ oz. gin
⅕ oz. vodka
⅕ oz. white rum
⅕ oz. tequila
⅕ oz. Grand Marnier
2 oz. lemon juice
2 oz. lime juice
1 oz. soda water

garnish: lemon wedge
Pour ingredients over ice into a highball glass. This recipe is simply a Long Island Iced Tea made with Grand Marnier. To

make a "Californian" version of many cocktails, substitute Grand Marnier for Cointreau or triple sec.

California Margarita

1 oz. tequila
½ oz. Grand Marnier
5 oz. lime juice
salt
garnish: lime wedge
Moisten and salt the glass's rim. For a frozen margarita, blend ingredients with ice. For a traditional margarita, shake ingredients and pour over ice cubes.

Canadian Cocktail

1½ oz. Canadian whiskey
½ oz. Cointreau or triple sec
½ tsp. fine sugar
bitters
Shake ingredients over ice. Strain into a martini glass.

Cape Cod

1½ oz. vodka
1 oz. lime juice
3 oz. cranberry juice
Build ingredients into a highball glass. Garnish with a lime wedge.

Caramel Kiss

1½ oz. butterscotch schnapps
½ oz. Baileys
½ oz. white rum
½ oz. brown crème de cacao
½ oz. Kahlúa
½ oz. pineapple juice

1 oz. cream
garnish: Hershey's Kiss or a caramel
Shake ingredients firmly with ice and strain into a martini glass, the rim of which has been moistened and garnished with a sprinkle of cocoa power. Lots of work. Lots of flavor.

Caramilk Martini

1 oz. vanilla vodka
1 oz. Baileys
½ oz. butterscotch schnapps
½ Caramilk chocolate bar
Microwave the Caramilk bar until melted (seconds). Stir up and drizzle mixture into a chilled martini glass, swirling into desired pattern. Re-chill. Shake remaining ingredients firmly with ice and strain into the prepared martini glass. Absolutely worth the effort!

Casablanca

1½ oz. white rum
½ oz. triple sec
3 oz. lime juice
dash of grenadine
garnish: cherry and orange slice
Blend ingredients thoroughly with ice. Serve in a large cocktail glass.

Chambord Royale

1 oz. vodka
1 oz. Chambord
1 oz. triple sec
2 oz. lime juice

Shake ingredients firmly with ice and strain into a martini glass. Garnish with a lemon twist.

Champagne Cocktail

1 demerara sugar cube
dash of Angostura bitters
½ oz. cognac
Champagne to fill
Place the sugar cube in a Champagne flute. Add bitters and cognac. Fill with Champagne. Squeeze the oils from a lemon twist into the glass and rub the twist around the rim. Drop in twist. Classic!

Champagne Fizz

1 oz. gin
1 oz. lemon juice
½ tsp. fine sugar
chilled Champagne
Shake the first three ingredients with ice. Strain into a Champagne flute and top with Champagne.

Chi Chi

1 oz. vodka
½ oz. coconut syrup
3 oz. pineapple juice
2 oz. cream
garnish: cherry and orange slice
Blend ingredients thoroughly.

Pour into a large cocktail glass. All bartenders hate making this time-consuming recipe. I retaliate by making a little extra for myself. See also **Piña Colada**

Chocolate Martini

1½ oz. Baileys
1 oz. vodka
1 oz. crème de cacao
Shake ingredients with ice and strain into a martini glass. Garnish with chocolate shavings. You'll rarely go wrong when offering your friends a Chocolate Martini.

Chocolate Monkey

1 oz. brown crème de cacao
1 oz. crème de banane
1 scoop vanilla ice cream
2 tsp. chocolate powder
1 banana (save a slice)
Blend ingredients until slushy, then pour into a chilled martini glass. Garnish with a banana slice.

Classic Cocktail

1½ oz. brandy
½ oz. Cointreau
2 oz. lemon juice
dash of grenadine
Shake ingredients with ice. Strain into a martini glass.

Coco Rum Yum

1 oz. Baileys
1 oz. coconut Malibu rum
1 oz. white crème de cacao

2 oz. cream
Shake ingredients with ice and pour into a rocks glass. Garnish with chocolate sprinkles.

Cosmopolitan Martini

1½ oz. vodka
½ oz. Cointreau
2 oz. lime juice
1 oz. cranberry juice
Shake ingredients with ice. Strain into a martini glass.

Crantini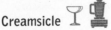

2 oz. cranberry vodka
½ oz. triple sec
1 oz. lime juice
2 oz. cranberry juice
Shake ingredients with ice and strain into a martini glass. The Crantini has many variations, so ask about personal preferences before mixing. Garnish with a lemon twist.

Creamsicle

1 oz. gin
1 oz. advocaat
2 oz. orange juice
1 oz. cream
garnish: orange slice and cherry
Blend ingredients thoroughly with ice. Serve in a large cocktail glass.

Cuba Libra

1 oz. dark rum
½ oz. lime juice
3 oz. Coke
garnish: lime

Pour ingredients over ice into rocks glass. This Cuban creation is over one hundred years old and is still popular. In the movie Cocktail, *a very busy Tom Cruise rifled through a cocktail guide (not* Mulligan's*) and was annoyed to discover that a Cuba Libra was nothing more than a "Rum and Coke!"*

Daiquiri

1 oz. white rum
3 oz. lime juice
garnish: lime
Blend ingredients thoroughly. Pour into a large cocktail glass. Make a Banana Daiquiri by adding ½ oz. of crème de banane and one half of a banana. Create a strawberry version by adding strawberries and strawberry liqueur.

Like the Cuba Libra, this recipe is over one hundred years old, is of Cuban descent and remains very popular today.

See also **Margarita**

Dirty Martini

2 oz. gin
¼ oz. dry vermouth
¼ oz. olive brine
"Dirty" refers to the added olive brine. I recommend that you stir the ingredients gently, together with very cold, hard ice, then strain into a martini glass.

Dirty Mother
1 oz. tequila
2 oz. Kahlúa
3 oz. milk
Pour ingredients over ice into a rocks glass. Originally this recipe was made with cream instead of milk. How times have changed!

Doctor Funk
1½ oz. dark rum
½ oz. Pernod
3 oz. lemon juice
2 oz. soda water
garnish: orange
Pour ingredients over ice into a highball glass.

Dog's Nose
1 oz. gin
1 pint beer
Pour the gin into a pint glass and fill with beer.

Dreamsicle
1 oz. Baileys
3 oz. orange juice
garnish: orange slice
Pour ingredients over ice into a rocks glass.

Dubonnet Cocktail
1 oz. gin
1 oz. Dubonnet
dash of bitters
garnish: lemon twist
Shake ingredients with ice. Strain into a martini glass.

Durkee Cocktail
1 oz. Appleton rum
½ oz. curaçao
1 oz. lemon juice
simple syrup to taste
Shake ingredients with ice and strain into a martini glass. Durkee is the name of a spice company from Buffalo, New York, which was founded in 1850; its products are popular in Jamaica.

Earthquake
½ oz. vodka
½ oz. gin
½ oz. green crème de menthe
Pour ingredients over ice into a rocks glass.

Eggnog
1 oz. vanilla vodka
½ oz. Baileys
½ oz. Irish whiskey
2 oz. cream
Shake ingredients firmly with ice and pour into a rocks glass. Garnish with a dusting of nutmeg.

El Diablo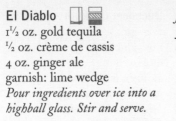

1½ oz. gold tequila
½ oz. crème de cassis
4 oz. ginger ale
garnish: lime wedge
Pour ingredients over ice into a highball glass. Stir and serve.

flow. Note the desirable yin and yang effects produced upon consumption.

Fiesta

1 oz. white rum

Evergreen

1 oz. tequila
½ oz. green crème de menthe
½ oz. Galliano
5 oz. pineapple juice
garnish: fresh mint
Pour ingredients over ice into a highball glass.

½ oz. Cointreau
5 oz. lemon juice
¼ oz. grenadine
Shake ingredients with ice. Strain into a martini glass.

Fifth Avenue

1½ oz. apricot brandy
½ oz. white crème de cacao
2 oz. cream
Shake ingredients with ice. Strain into a martini glass.

Feng Shui

½ oz. vodka
½ oz. gin
½ oz. rum
½ oz. triple sec
1 oz. lemon juice
1 oz. lime juice
1 oz. soda water
Shake quickly with ice and strain into a martini glass. Garnish with citrus twists. Place the symmetrical martini upon the bar's surface along the imaginary line perpendicular to the recipient's chest, within easy reach, assuring maximum chi

Flirt-Tini

1½ oz. raspberry vodka
½ oz. triple sec
½ oz. lime juice
½ oz. cranberry juice
½ oz. pineapple juice
Shake ingredients with ice and strain into a martini glass. Garnish with fruit slices.

Fluffy Duck

1 oz. gin
1/2 oz. advocaat
1/2 oz. Cointreau
3 oz. orange juice
*Blend ingredients thoroughly
with ice. Pour into a large
cocktail glass.*

Frangelico Crush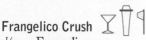

1 1/2 oz. Frangelico
1/2 oz. Grand Marnier
3 oz. orange juice
*Shake ingredients with ice and
strain into a martini glass.*

Freddy Fudpucker

1 1/2 oz. tequila
1/2 oz. Galliano
2 oz. orange juice
*Shake ingredients with ice and
strain into a martini glass.
Garnish with an orange slice.*

Friar Tuck

2 oz. Frangelico
2 oz. lemon juice
dashes of grenadine
*Shake ingredients with ice and
strain into a martini glass.
Garnish with a lemon wedge.*

Funky Monkey

1 oz. Baileys
1/2 oz. Kahlúa
1/2 oz. crème de banane
1 banana
4 oz. milk
coconut syrup
vanilla ice cream (optional)

*Blend ingredients thoroughly
with ice. Pour into a large
cocktail glass.*

Fuzzy Navel

1 oz. peach schnapps
3 oz. orange juice
*Pour ingredients over ice into a
highball glass. Add an ounce of
vodka for an extra punch.*

Gibson

1 3/4 oz. gin
1/2 oz. dry vermouth
garnish: cocktail onion
*If you can make a martini, you
can make a Gibson. Simply stir
ingredients with ice to chill and
strain into a martini glass.*

Eat, drink, and be merry,
for tomorrow they may
cancel your VISA.
  Anonymous

Gimlet

1 1/2 oz. gin
1/2 oz. triple sec
3 oz. lime juice
*Shake ingredients with ice.
Strain into a martini glass.*

Gin Alexander
See *Alexander*

Gin Cocktail

2 oz. gin
dash of bitters

41

Shake ingredients with ice. Strain into a martini glass.

Gin Fizz
1 oz. gin
1 oz. lemon juice
¼ tsp. fine sugar
4 oz. soda water
Shake and strain the gin, juice and sugar over ice into a highball glass. Top off with soda water.

Ginger Spice
1 oz. spiced rum
4 oz. ginger ale
Pour ingredients over ice into a highball glass.

Gin Ricky
1 oz. gin
4 oz. soda water
garnish: lime wedge
Only the name is fancy. This is just a gin and soda garnished with a lime wedge. A little squeeze of fresh lime is a nice touch.

Glogg
1 part port
1 part sherry
1 part brandy
1 part whiskey
cardamom to taste
cinnamon to taste
allspice to taste
Microwave ingredients at a low setting to let the flavors develop. Serve in a mug. Traditionally,

blanched almonds and raisins are added. You decide!

Glühwein
5 oz. red wine
2 oz. orange juice
1 lemon slice
1 orange slice
½ cinnamon stick
2 cloves
¼ tsp. sugar
garnish: cinnamon stick
Microwave ingredients at a low setting to let the flavors develop. Serve in a mug garnished with a cinnamon stick.

Godfather
1½ oz. Scotch
½ oz. Amaretto
Pour ingredients over ice into a rocks glass.

Godmother
1½ oz. vodka
½ oz. Amaretto
Pour ingredients over ice into a rocks glass.

Golden Cadillac
1 oz. Galliano
1 oz. white crème de cacao
2 oz. milk
Shake ingredients with ice. Strain into a martini glass.

Gorgeous George
1 oz. Baileys

1 oz. Grand Marnier
2 oz. cream
Shake ingredients with ice and strain into a martini glass.

Grape Kool-Aid
1½ oz. Chambord
½ oz. vodka
½ oz. triple sec
4 oz. cranberry juice
Shake ingredients with ice. Strain into a highball glass filled with ice.

Grasshopper
1½ oz. green crème de menthe
½ oz. white crème de cacao
2 oz. cream
Shake ingredients with ice. Strain into a martini glass. My favorite Christmas drink.

Greek Coffee
½ oz. Metaxa
½ oz. ouzo
coffee
whipped cream
garnish: cherry
Moisten and sugar mug's rim. Pour liqueurs and coffee. Top with whipped cream and a dash of Kahlúa.

Green-Eyed Monster
1 oz. Baileys
1 oz. green Chartreuse
1 oz. sweet vermouth
Shake ingredients with ice and strain into a martini glass.

Greyhound
1 oz. vodka
5 oz. grapefruit juice
garnish: lemon wedge
Pour ingredients over ice into a large highball glass.

I have made an important discovery—that alcohol, taken in sufficient quantities, produces all the effects of intoxication.
Oscar Wilde

Grog
2 oz. dark rum
1 tsp. brown sugar
2–3 cloves
1 cinnamon stick
garnish: lemon wedge
Add ingredients to a mug and fill with hot water. Let the mixture steep for a minute.

Harvey Wallbanger
1 oz. vodka
½ oz. Galliano
5 oz. orange juice
garnish: orange slice
Pour vodka and orange juice over ice. Float Galliano on top.

Havana Cocktail
1 oz. rum
3 oz. pineapple juice
1 oz. lime juice
Shake ingredients with ice and strain into a martini glass.

Honolulu Hammer
1 oz. vodka
½ oz. Amaretto
3 oz. pineapple juice
dash of grenadine
Shake ingredients with ice.
Strain into a martini glass.

Hooch
1 oz. grain alcohol
4 oz. Kool-Aid
Pour ingredients over ice into a
highball glass. Party "Prohibition-
style" with this concoction.

Hot Buttered Rum
1 oz. dark rum
1 tsp. brown sugar
1 tsp. butter
4 oz. hot water
cloves to taste
cinnamon to taste
vanilla extract to taste
honey to taste
garnish: cinnamon stick and
    lemon wedge
Mix ingredients with hot water.

Hurricane
1 oz. light rum
1 oz. dark rum
1 oz. Alizé or 1 oz. passion
    fruit syrup
1 oz. lime juice
Shake ingredients with ice.
Strain into a martini glass.

Hypnotini
2 oz. Hypnotiq
1 oz. vodka

½ oz. lemon juice
garnish: lemon twist
Shake ingredients with ice and
strain into a martini glass. This
tropical blue sensation is sure to
put you in a trance.

Incredible Hulk
2 oz. Hypnotiq
2 oz. Hennessy cognac
Shake ingredients with ice and
strain into a martini glass.

Insomniac
1½ oz. tequila
2 oz. Red Bull
1 oz. orange juice
dash of grenadine
garnish: small cup of espresso
    beans on the side
Shake ingredients with ice and
strain into a martini glass.

Irish Coffee
1½ oz. Irish whiskey
½ oz. Kahlúa
coffee
whipped cream
garnish: cherry
Moisten and sugar mug's rim.
Pour liqueurs and coffee. Top
with whipped cream and a dash
of Kahlúa.

Jägermeister Mule
1 oz. vodka
½ oz. lime juice
½ oz. simple syrup
dash of Angostura bitters
3 oz. ginger beer

1 oz. Jägermeister
garnish: squeezed lime
Shake first four ingredients with ice and strain into an ice-filled highball glass. Top with ginger beer and Jäger.

Jägermonster
1 oz. Jägermeister
4 oz. orange juice
dash of grenadine
Shake ingredients with ice. Strain into a martini glass.

Jamaican Coffee
1 oz. Jamaican rum
¼ oz. Tia Maria
coffee
whipped cream
garnish: cherry
Moisten and sugar mug's rim. Pour liqueurs and coffee. Top with whipped cream and a dash of Tia Maria. Try this and you'll be jammin' too.

Jamaican Me Crazy
1 oz. Jamaican rum
½ oz. triple sec
3 oz. pineapple juice
1 oz. lime juice
mango (if available)
Blend ingredients thoroughly with ice. Serve in a large cocktail glass. Cool runnings.

John Collins

1 oz. whiskey
3 oz. lemon juice
2 oz. soda water
garnish: cherry and orange slice
Pour ingredients over ice into a highball glass.

Kamikaze
1½ oz. vodka
½ oz. triple sec
1 oz. lime juice
garnish: lemon slice
Shake ingredients with ice and strain into a martini glass.

Key Lime Martini
2 oz. vanilla vodka
1 oz. lime juice
½ oz. pineapple juice
½ oz. milk
garnish: lemon slice
Shake ingredients with ice and strain into a martini glass.

Killer Kool-Aid
⅓ oz. vodka
⅓ oz. Amaretto
⅓ oz. melon liqueur
2 oz. cranberry juice
2 oz. 7UP
garnish: lemon wedge
Shake first four ingredients with ice and strain into a martini glass. Top with 7UP. Classic!

Kir
¼ oz. crème de cassis
5 oz. white wine
Pour crème de cassis into a wine glass. Top with wine.

Pour ingredients over ice into a highball glass.

Lager and Lime
1 pint lager
2 oz. lime juice
Pour a lager and top with lime juice. If available, use Rose's Lime Cordial.

Kir Royale
¼ oz. crème de cassis
5 oz. Champagne
Prepare as you would a Kir, but move up to Champagne.

Lava Lamp
2 oz. vodka
2 oz. raspberry liqueur
1 tsp. liquid honey
Shake first two ingredients with ice and strain into a well-chilled martini glass. Slowly tip the spoonful of honey into the martini. Your guests will be impressed by how closely this martini resembles the original Lava Lamp.

Kiss Me Quickly
1 oz. Pernod
¼ oz. curaçao
dash of Angostura bitters
3 oz. soda water
garnish: lemon slice
Shake first three ingredients with ice and strain into a martini glass. Top with soda.

Lemon Drop
1½ oz. vodka
½ oz. triple sec
½ oz. lemon juice
½ oz. lime juice
garnish: lemon and lime twists
Shake ingredients with ice and strain into a martini glass.

Weaseling out of things is important to learn. It's what separates us from the animals ... except the weasel.
  Homer Simpson

Long Island Iced Tea
⅕ oz. gin
⅕ oz. vodka
⅕ oz. white rum
⅕ oz. tequila
⅕ oz. triple sec
  or
1 oz. Long Island mix

Klondike Cooler
1 oz. Canadian whiskey
3 oz. ginger ale
2 oz. soda water
garnish: cherry

2 oz. lemon juice
2 oz. lime juice
1 oz. Coke
garnish: lemon wedge
Pour ingredients into a tall highball glass. If you substitute Grand Marnier for triple sec, you will have an "Electric" Long Island Iced Tea.

Lynchburg Lemonade
1 oz. Jack Daniel's
½ oz. triple sec
2 oz. lemon juice
2 oz. 7UP
garnish: lemon wedge
Pour ingredients over ice into a highball glass.

Madison's Malibu
1 oz. Malibu rum
½ oz. blue curaçao
3 oz. pineapple juice
1 oz. lime juice
garnish: lemon wedge
Pour ingredients over ice into a highball glass. Stir gently. If you happen to be in Calgary, drop by Madison's and I or co-creator Evan Truman will make you one.

Mai Tai
1 oz. dark rum
1 oz. white rum
½ oz. triple sec or Cointreau
½ oz. Amaretto
3 oz. orange juice
2 oz. lime juice
¼ oz. grenadine

Shake ingredients with ice. Pour into a tall highball glass. If you happen to have orgeat syrup (and who doesn't?), you can substitute it for Amaretto.

Manhattan
1½ oz. whiskey
½ oz. sweet or dry vermouth
dash of bitters
garnish: cherry
Shake ingredients with ice. Strain into a martini glass. A perfect Manhattan calls for equal parts of sweet and dry vermouths.

Margarita
1½ oz. tequila
½ oz. triple sec
3 oz. lime juice
garnish: lime wedge
Frozen method: Blend ingredients into a slush and pour into a tall highball glass. Original method: Shake ingredients and strain into a martini glass or over ice. In either case, salt the glass's rim.
See also **Daiquiri**

Martini, The Original
2½ oz. gin
¼ to ½ oz. dry vermouth
A consensus never has been, nor ever will be, reached on how to make a martini properly. All I can do is give you the basics: (1) obtain the desired amount of

each ingredient, preferably more gin than vermouth, (2) shake, stir or simply introduce them to each other, (3) pour the result into a martini glass over ice, or not, (4) garnish with any number of olives, a twist or nothing at all, and (5) claim to have made the greatest martini since its invention over one hundred years ago.
Cheers . . . and good luck!

Mary
See **Bloody Mary**

Matador
1 oz. tequila
3 oz. pineapple juice
3 oz. lemon juice
garnish: lime wedge
Shake ingredients with ice. Pour into a tall highball glass.

Mathematician's Martini
(log(100) base 10) oz. vanilla vodka
(8! - 40320) oz. Baileys
$[(\sin(45)+\sin(45)+0.858)]$ oz. Kahlúa
(x/y) oz. cream, where $x=50$, $y=25$
Calculate proportions. Sum ingredients. Randomize result. Store in memory. Clear.

Melon Ball
1 oz. melon liqueur
$^{1}/_{2}$ oz. vodka

4 oz. orange juice
2 oz. 7UP
garnish: orange slice
Shake ingredients with ice. Pour into a tall highball glass.

Mexican Coffee
$1^{1}/_{2}$ oz. tequila
$^{1}/_{2}$ oz. Kahlúa
coffee
whipped cream
Pour tequila, Kahlúa and coffee into a mug. Top with whipped cream and a dash of Kahlúa.

Midori Cocktail
1 oz. Midori or melon liqueur
4 oz. chilled Champagne
Pour Midori into a Champagne flute and top with Champagne.

Millionaire
$1^{1}/_{2}$ oz. whiskey
$^{1}/_{2}$ oz. Cointreau or triple sec
dash of grenadine
Shake ingredients with ice. Strain into a martini glass.

Mimosa

¹/₂ oz. Cointreau or triple sec
4 oz. chilled Champagne
3 oz. orange juice
Pour ingredients into a chilled Champagne flute.

Minted Mocha

1 oz. peppermint schnapps
1 cup hot chocolate
whipped cream
Stir schnapps into hot chocolate. Top with whipped cream and a dusting of chocolate powder.

Mintini

1 oz. vodka
1 oz. green crème de menthe
Shake ingredients with ice. Strain into a martini glass.

Mint Julep

several mint leaves
1 oz. simple syrup
dash of Angostura bitters
crushed ice
2 oz. bourbon
Muddle first three ingredients and pour into highball glass, with ice to fill. Add bourbon and stir. Replace simple syrup with demerara sugar when possible.

Mobay

1¹/₂ oz. Appleton rum
¹/₂ oz. Tia Maria
1 oz. coconut milk
Montego Bay, Jamaica, is the inspiration for this martini, which should be shaken firmly and strained into a well-chilled martini glass. Shout-out to Buju Banton: thanks for the dancehall music!

Mojito

2-4 lime wedges
½ oz. simple syrup
several mint leaves
crushed ice
soda water to fill
2 oz. dark rum
garnish: mint sprig
Muddle the first three ingredients and pour into a tall glass. Add rum and soda water. Stir. Simply perfect!

Monkey's Lunch

1¹/₂ oz. Kahlúa
¹/₂ oz. crème de banane
3 oz. milk
garnish: cherry
Pour ingredients over ice into a rocks glass.

Monk's Coffee

¹/₄ oz. Swiss chocolate almond liqueur
¹/₄ oz. Grand Marnier
¹/₄ oz. Frangelico
¹/₄ oz. crème de cacao
coffee
whipped cream
garnish: cherry
Moisten and sugar mug's rim. Pour liqueurs and coffee. Top with whipped cream and a dash of Grand Marnier.

Monte Cristo

1½ oz. Grand Marnier
½ oz. Kahlúa
coffee
whipped cream
garnish: cherry
*Moisten and sugar snifter's rim.
Pour liqueurs and coffee. Top
with whipped cream and a dash
of Kahlúa.*

Moscow Mule

1 oz. vodka
5 oz. ginger beer
garnish: lime wedge
*Pour ingredients over ice into a
highball glass.*

Mudslide

1 oz. vodka
1 oz. Kahlúa
1 oz. Baileys
*Blend ingredients thoroughly with
ice. Pour into a large cocktail glass.*

Mulligan's Martini

3 oz. vanilla vodka
garnish: lemon twist.
*Shake vodka firmly with ice, to
chill and dilute slightly—small ice
crystals should form. Pour into a
very well chilled martini glass, the
rim of which has been dressed with
the oils of a fresh lemon twist.*

Mustang

½ oz. vodka
5 oz. Champagne
garnish: orange
*Pour ingredients over ice into a
highball glass.*

Nutcracker

½ oz. vodka
½ oz. Kahlúa
½ oz. Baileys
½ oz. Amaretto
*Shake ingredients with ice.
Strain into a martini glass.*

Very funny, Scotty.
Now beam up my clothes.
  Bumper sticker

Nutty Banana

1 oz. Malibu rum
½ oz. crème de banane
½ oz. Frangelico
2 oz. cream
*Shake ingredients with ice and
strain into a martini glass.*

Nutty Russian

1 oz. vanilla vodka
1 oz. Frangelico
3 oz. cream
*Blend ingredients thoroughly
with ice. Pour into a large
cocktail glass. Thanks to Lorrie
Chute for this tasty gem!*

Old Fashioned

1 oz. rye
1 sugar cube
dash of bitters
2 oz. soda water
garnish: cherry, lemon and
  lime twists
*Combine the rye, sugar and
bitters. Top with soda water.*

Olympic Cocktail

1 oz. brandy
1 oz. Cointreau or triple sec
2 oz. orange juice
Shake ingredients with ice.
Strain into a martini glass.

Orange Blossom

2 oz. gin
2 oz. orange juice
garnish: orange slice.
Shake ingredients with ice and strain into a martini glass.

Orangesicle

2 oz. orange vodka
1/2 oz. Amaretto
1/2 oz. Grand Marnier
2 oz. orange juice
2 oz. cream
garnish: orange twists.
Shake ingredients with ice and strain into a martini glass.

Paralyzer

1 1/2 oz. tequila or vodka
1/2 oz. Kahlúa
3 oz. Coke
2 oz. cream
Pour the ingredients over ice into a large highball glass. Pour the Coke before the cream or you will end up with a fizzing mess. Just try it!

Parisian Cocktail

1 1/2 oz. gin
1/4 oz. dry vermouth
1/4 oz. crème de cassis
Shake ingredients with ice.
Strain into a martini glass.

Pi

3.0000000000 oz. gin
0.1415926536 oz. dry vermouth
Shake, then round up and strain into a chilled martini glass.
Garnish with approximately
π *olives.*

Piña Colada

1 oz. rum
1/2 oz. coconut syrup
3 oz. pineapple juice
2 oz. cream
garnish: orange slice and cherry
Blend ingredients thoroughly with ice and pour into a large cocktail glass.
    See also **Chi Chi**

Imagination is more
important than knowledge.
   Albert Einstein

Pineapple Pushover

1 oz. crème de cacao
1/2 oz. Amaretto
3 oz. pineapple juice
2 oz. milk
Blend ingredients thoroughly with ice. Pour into a large cocktail glass.

Pink Lady

1 1/2 oz. gin
1/2 oz. cherry brandy
2 oz. cream
1/4 oz. grenadine
Blend ingredients thoroughly with ice. Pour into a martini glass.

Pink Squirrel

1 oz. Amaretto
1 oz. crème de cacao
2 oz. cream
Blend ingredients
thoroughly with ice.
Pour into a martini glass.

Pisco Sour

2 oz. pisco brandy
1 oz. lemon juice
dashes of simple syrup
2–3 drops of Angostura bitters
Shake ingredients with ice and
strain into a martini glass. You
may substitute another brandy
for the pisco if desired.

One more drink
and I'll be under the host.
   Dorothy Parker

Planter's Punch

1 oz. white rum
1 oz. dark rum
2 oz. orange juice
2 oz. lime juice
garnish: orange slice and cherry
Shake ingredients with ice. Pour
into a large highball glass.

Polar Bear

1 oz. Baileys
4 oz. hot chocolate
whipped cream
Combine Baileys and hot choco-
late. Top with whipped cream.

Polo Cocktail

2 oz. gin
1½ oz. lemon juice
1½ oz. orange juice
Shake ingredients with ice.
Strain into a martini glass.

Popsicle

1 oz. vodka
½ oz. Parfait Amour
½ oz. Amaretto
2 oz. lime juice
2 oz. 7UP
garnish: lemon wedge
Shake ingredients with ice. Pour
into a large highball glass.

Port Cocktail

1½ oz. port
½ oz. brandy
Shake ingredients with ice.
Strain into a martini glass.

Programmer's Martini

```
10: long int tequila
20: short int triple_sec
30: long_int garnish =
lime_wedge
40: constant float
pink_grapefruit
50: garnish = lemon_wedge
60: for(i=room temperature1; i
<= chilled; i++)
70: shake_ingredients();
80: strain_ingredients();
9: for(i=full glass1; i <=
consumed; i++)
100:enjoy_martini(enjoy_mart
ini());
/*  Author: Shawn Mulligan
    Purpose: Recursive Fun  */
```

Purple Haze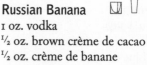

1 oz. white rum
½ oz. Chambord
½ oz. curaçao
1 oz. pineapple juice
3 oz. orange juice
garnish: orange slice and
 cherry
*Shake ingredients with ice. Pour
into a large highball glass.*

Reminds me of my safari in
Africa. Somebody forgot the
corkscrew and for several
days we had nothing to live
on but food and water.
 W.C. Fields

Rob Roy

1½ oz. Scotch
½ oz. sweet vermouth
garnish: lemon twist or cherry
*Shake ingredients with ice.
Strain into a martini glass.*

Rocket Fuel

½ oz. vodka
½ oz. triple sec
½ oz. white rum
½ oz. gin
½ oz. tequila
*Shake ingredients with ice.
Strain into a martini glass.*

Root Beer

See ***Bartender's Root Beer***

Roy Rogers

4 oz. cola
2 oz. lime juice
¼ oz. grenadine
garnish: orange slice and
 cherry
*Pour ingredients over ice into a
large cocktail glass.*

Russian Banana

1 oz. vodka
½ oz. brown crème de cacao
½ oz. crème de banane
2 oz. cream
*Shake ingredients with ice and
pour into a rocks glass.*

Russian Cocktail

1 oz. vodka
1 oz. Kahlúa
*Shake ingredients with ice.
Strain into a martini glass.*

Rusty Nail

1½ oz. Scotch
½ oz. Drambuie
garnish: cherry
*Pour ingredients over ice into a
rocks glass.*

Saktini

1 oz. gin
½ oz. sake
garnish: olives
*Shake ingredients with ice.
Strain into a martini glass.*

Salty Dog

1 oz. vodka
5 oz. grapefruit juice
garnish: lemon wedge
Salt the glass's rim. Pour ingredients over ice into a large highball glass. This is simply a Greyhound with a salted rim.

Samtini

1 oz. vodka
½ oz. white sambuca
½ blue curaçao
Shake ingredients with ice. Strain into a martini glass.

Sangria

1 oz. brandy
½ oz. triple sec or Cointreau
½ oz. port or sherry
3 oz. red wine
2 oz. orange juice
2 oz. soda water
garnish: orange, lemon, lime slices
Pour ingredients over ice into a large highball glass.

Scarlett O'Hara

1 oz. Southern Comfort
3 oz. lime juice
¼ oz. grenadine
Shake ingredients with ice. Strain into a martini glass.

Scooby Snack

1 oz. vodka
1 oz. Frangelico
1 oz. Baileys
2 oz. cream
garnish: dollop of whipped cream
Shake ingredients with ice and strain into a martini glass. (Zoinks! Yes. Good.)

Scorpion

1 oz. white rum
½ oz. brandy
½ oz. Amaretto
3 oz. orange juice
2 oz. lemon juice
garnish: orange slice and cherry
Blend ingredients thoroughly with ice. Pour into a large cocktail glass.

Scotch Mist

2 oz. Scotch
crushed ice
Pour Scotch over crushed ice. To crush ice, wrap a few cubes in a dinner napkin and smash them against the bar.

Screwdriver

1 oz. vodka
5 oz. orange juice
garnish: orange slice
Pour ingredients over ice into a large highball glass.

Sea Breeze

1 oz. vodka
2 oz. cranberry juice
2 oz. grapefruit juice
garnish: squeezed lime
    wedges.
Shake ingredients with ice and pour into a highball glass.

Sex on the Beach

1 oz. vodka
1 oz. peach schnapps
3 oz. orange juice
dash of grenadine
garnish: lime wedges
Build ingredients into a highball glass. Stir.

Shandy

10 oz. draft beer
2–3 oz. ginger ale
Pour ginger ale atop the draft beer.

Shanghai Sling

1 oz. whiskey
3 oz. orange juice
2 oz. lemon juice
1/4 oz. grenadine
garnish: orange slice and cherry
Pour ingredients over ice into a large highball glass.

Shirley Templetini Mocktini

2 oz. orange juice
1 oz. lime juice
2 oz. Sprite
dash of grenadine
garnish: orange slice and a
    maraschino cherry

Shake ingredients with ice and strain into a martini glass.

Side Car

1 1/2 oz. brandy
1/2 oz. triple sec or Cointreau
2 oz. lemon juice
Shake ingredients with ice. Strain into a martini glass.

Silver Cloud

1 1/2 oz. white crème de menthe
1/2 oz. Amaretto
2 oz. cream
Blend ingredients thoroughly with ice. Pour into a martini glass.

Singapore Sling

1 oz. gin
1/2 oz. cherry brandy
2 oz. orange juice
2 oz. lemon juice
1 oz. soda water
garnish: orange and lemon
    slices
Pour all ingredients except cherry brandy over ice into a tall highball glass. Float cherry brandy on top. The orange juice is optional.

Sloe Dog

1 oz. sloe gin
5 oz. grapefruit juice
garnish: lemon wedge
Pour ingredients over ice into a large highball glass.
This recipe is simply a Greyhound using sloe gin instead of vodka.

Sloe Gin Fizz

1 oz. sloe gin
2 oz. lemon juice
3 oz. soda water
garnish: lemon wedge
Pour ingredients over ice into a highball glass. You can add a little fine sugar to sweeten the mix, if desired.

Snowball

1 oz. advocaat
3 oz. lemon juice
2 oz. Sprite
Blend ingredients thoroughly with ice. Pour into a large cocktail glass.

Spanish Coffee

1 oz. brandy
½ oz. Kahlúa
coffee
whipped cream
garnish: cherry
Moisten and sugar mug's rim. Pour liqueurs and coffee. Top with whipped cream and a dash of Kahlúa.

People who think they know everything are a great annoyance to those of us who do.
Anonymous

Spritzer

4 oz. white wine
3 oz. soda water
garnish: lemon wedge
Pour ingredients over ice into a highball glass.

Stinger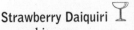

1 oz. brandy
1 oz. white crème de menthe
garnish: cherry
Pour ingredients over ice into a rocks glass. Especially good over crushed ice.

Strawberry Daiquiri

1 oz. white rum
3 oz. lime juice
several strawberries
garnish: lime wedge
Blend ingredients thoroughly with ice. Pour into a large cocktail glass.

Sunburst
See **Mimosa**

Tequila Matador

1 oz. tequila
3 oz. pineapple juice
1 oz. lime juice
Shake ingredients with ice. Strain into a chilled Champagne flute.

Tequila Sunrise

1 oz. tequila
5 oz. orange juice
¼ oz. grenadine
garnish: orange wedge
Pour ingredients over ice into a highball glass.

Tequini

1½ oz. tequila
½ oz. dry vermouth

dash of bitters
garnish: lemon twist
Shake ingredients with ice.
Strain into a martini glass.

Thug Passion

2 oz. Alizé or passion fruit syrup
2 oz. Champagne
Pour ingredients over ice into a
rocks glass.

Tim-Tini Martini

1 oz. Baileys
1 oz. Tia Maria
½ oz. vanilla vodka
¼ tsp. instant coffee
¼ tsp. sugar
garnish: sprinkle of powdered
sugar and a cream-filled
Timbit on the side
Shake ingredients firmly with
ice and strain into a chilled
martini glass.

Titanic

1 oz. vodka
½ oz. Galliano
½ oz. Parfait Amour
Shake ingredients with ice.
Strain into a martini glass.

Tom Collins

1 oz. gin
3 oz. lemon juice
2 oz. soda water
garnish: lemon wedge
Pour ingredients over ice into a
highball glass. Add a little fine
sugar if desired.

Top Banana

1 oz. crème de banane
1 oz. vodka
3 oz. orange juice
Shake ingredients with ice. Pour
into a rocks glass.

Trailer Park Summer

2 oz. Southern Comfort
3 oz. cherry Kool-Aid
garnish: leftovers
Shake ingredients with ice and
strain into a martini glass.

Vanilla Coke

1½ oz. vanilla vodka
3 oz. Coke
Build ingredients over ice into a
rocks glass.

Velvet Hammer

1 oz. vodka
½ oz. white crème de cacao
½ oz. Kahlúa
2 oz. cream
Shake ingredients thoroughly
with ice. Pour into a martini
glass.

Waldorf

1 oz. bourbon
½ oz. Pernod
½ oz. sweet vermouth
dash of bitters
Shake ingredients with ice.
Strain into a martini glass.

Ward Eight

1 oz. whiskey or bourbon
1 oz. orange juice
1 oz. lemon juice
1/4 oz. grenadine
garnish: lemon twist
*Shake ingredients with ice.
Strain into a martini glass.*

Watermelon Cooler

1 oz. strawberry liqueur
1/2 oz. vodka
1/2 oz. triple sec
3 oz. orange juice
1 oz. lime juice
garnish: lemon wedge
*Pour ingredients over ice into a
highball glass.*

Whiskey Sour

2 oz. rye
3 oz. lemon juice
garnish: lemon
*Shake ingredients with ice.
Strain into a martini glass.*

White Russian

1 1/2 oz. vodka
1/2 oz. Kahlúa
3 oz. milk
*Pour ingredients over ice into a
rocks glass.*

White Wine Spritzer
See *Spritzer*

Woo Woo

1 oz. vodka
1 oz. peach schnapps
1 oz. cranberry juice
lime wedge
*Shake ingredients with ice and
strain into a martini glass that
has been rimmed with the lime
wedge. Squeeze and drop lime
into glass.*

Zombie

1 oz. light rum
1 oz. dark rum
1 oz. amber rum
1/2 oz. Amaretto
1/2 oz. Alizé or passion fruit
  syrup
2 oz. lemon juice
2 oz. orange juice
1 oz. soda water
1/4 oz. grenadine
garnish: orange slice and
  cherry

Blend ingredients thoroughly with ice. Pour into a large high-ball glass. There are many variations on this recipe, perhaps because it has been circulating for over half a century. You might float some overproof rum on top, or add your favorite liqueur. We all know, however, that people order the Zombie for the three ounces of rum and not for the juices.

SHOOTERS

There is something about the downing of an assorted ounce of the world's finest liqueurs in a fraction of a second that brings a thrill and sense of satisfaction to most.

It took crafty Canuck bartenders to mold these tasty little gems into the barroom phenomenon of the 80s. Sure, the aromatic vapors of a fire-warmed Grand Marnier are nice, if you have the time, but make mine a B-52.

What do frozen fish, basketball, instant mashed potatoes and shooters have in common? They are all Canadian inventions ... and I think that you will agree, the shooter is the most significant.

There are literally millions of shooter combination possibilities, and it's your job and mine to find the most delicious. So get to it, and tell me what you find.

METHODOLOGY

The recipes in this section
list their ingredients in the correct order
for layering; therefore, you need only follow
this simple formula to succeed:

20% SKILL + 80% PATIENCE = 100% PERFECTION

Slowly pour the liqueurs over a maraschino cherry
or the rounded surface of a small spoon.
Chilling the shot glass (unless a larger glass is specified)
ahead of time will also help in layering.

If your recipe calls for shaking, don't over-shake.
This will only spoil the final product.
Basically, all you want to do is
mix and chill the
ingredients.

Enjoy!

A bartender
is just a pharmacist
with a limited inventory.
Bumper sticker

Aardvark
⅓ oz. Kahlúa
⅓ oz. Parfait Amour
⅓ oz. cream

ABC
⅓ oz. Amaretto
⅓ oz. Baileys
⅓ oz. Cointreau

Abstract Art
⅖ oz. Baileys
⅖ oz. vodka
⅕ oz. Parfait Amour
⅕ oz. brown crème de cacao
⅕ oz. grenadine
Shake the Baileys and vodka together. Strain the curdled mixture into a 2 oz. shot glass. Free-pour the remaining ingredients through the curds, creating a "sand-art" effect.

After Eight
⅓ oz. Kahlúa
⅓ oz. green crème de menthe
⅓ oz. Baileys

Alley Oop
⅓ oz. vodka
⅓ oz. apricot brandy
⅓ oz. cream

Alpine Avalanche
⅓ oz. Swiss chocolate almondliqueur
⅓ oz. Baileys
⅓ oz. Grand Marnier

Altered States
⅓ oz. Kahlúa
⅓ oz. pear liqueur
⅓ oz. Baileys

AMF
½ oz. Amaretto
½ oz. tequila

Angel's Tip
¾ oz. brown crème de cacao
¼ oz. cream

Apocalypse Now
⅓ oz. Baileys
⅓ oz. dry vermouth
⅓ oz. tequila
Pour the Baileys into the vermouth and tequila. Nasty!

Arctic Front
½ oz. Yukon Jack
½ oz. vodka

Atomic Bomb
½ oz. rye
½ oz. tequila

B-51
⅓ oz. Kahlúa
⅓ oz. Baileys
⅓ oz. Cointreau

B-52
⅓ oz. Kahlúa
⅓ oz. Baileys
⅓ oz. Grand Marnier

*The B-52 was invented in 1977
at the Keg restaurant in
Calgary, making it one of the
first shooters. Refrigerate the
Baileys first to achieve a cleaner
layer between the Grand
Marnier and Baileys.*

B-53
⅓ oz. Kahlúa
⅓ oz. Baileys
⅓ oz. peppermint schnapps

B-50-YOU!
⅓ oz. Kahlúa
⅓ oz. Baileys
⅓ oz. whatever!

*Choose whatever you like for the
top layer and give it a name.
Everybody's doing it.*

Bachelor's Surprise
⅓ oz. Kahlúa
⅓ oz. white crème de cacao
⅓ oz. Southern Comfort

Banana Bliss
¾ oz. crème de banane
¼ oz. cognac

Banana Split
⅓ oz. Kahlúa
⅓ oz. crème de banane
⅓ oz. cherry brandy or
    cherry whiskey

*Layer liqueurs and top with
whipped cream. Drizzle with
strawberry syrup or grenadine. Yum!*

Nudge, nudge, wink, wink,
say no more, know what I
mean ...
    "Monty Python's
        Flying Circus"

B & B
½ oz. Bénédictine
½ oz. brandy

*Just in case you don't have a
bottle of B & B handy.*

Bazooka Joe
⅖ oz. crème de banane
⅖ oz. Baileys
⅕ oz. Parfait Amour

*This is my favorite shooter. I like
to garnish mine with a Bazooka
Joe comic wrapped around the
glass and held with an elastic.*

Beer Bong

funnel, 7–8 inches in diameter
clear, flexible hose, 2–2.5 × 1
  in diameter
hose clamp
1–2 cans of beer
mop
camera

*Construction: Thoroughly clean
all parts. Slide hose over the tube
of funnel and secure with clamp.
For video instructions, go to
YouTube and look under "beer
bong." Application: Plug the end
of the hose with your thumb and
hold it above the funnel, essen-
tially clamping the hose from the
funnel. Fill the funnel with
beer. Slowly raise the funnel and
lower the hose, allowing the air
in the hose to be replaced with
beer—bubbles will escape. Place
the hose end in your mouth.
Release your thumb. Enjoy. Oh
yes—have a mop and camera
handy.*

Belize Breeze

½ oz. tequila
½ oz. Amaretto

Big Roller

⅓ oz. Kahlúa
⅓ oz. crème de banane
⅓ oz. Amaretto
garnish: cherry slice

Bikini

⅓ oz. strawberry liqueur
⅓ oz. Grand Marnier
⅓ oz. vodka

Black Banana

⅓ oz. Kahlúa
⅓ oz. crème de banane
⅓ oz. vodka

Black Bean

½ oz. anisette
½ oz. Parfait Amour or
  blue curaçao
dash of grenadine

Black Cat

1/3 oz. Kahlúa
1/3 oz. anisette
1/3 oz. tequila

Black Forest Cake

1/3 oz. Kahlúa
1/3 oz. cherry brandy
1/3 oz. Baileys

Black Jack

1/2 oz. tequila
1/2 oz. chocolate almond
   liqueur

Black Tie

1/3 oz. Parfait Amour
1/3 oz. Drambuie
1/3 oz. Scotch

Blow Job

1/2 oz. Kahlúa
1/2 oz. Baileys
whipped cream
Pour liqueurs into shot glass and top with whipped cream. Some substitute Amaretto for Baileys.

Blue Eyes

1/4 oz. crème de banane
1/4 oz. Parfait Amour
1/4 oz. vodka
1/4 oz. Scotch

Blue Hawaii

1/2 oz. Parfait Amour
1/2 oz. coconut rum

Blue Ice

1/3 oz. white crème de menthe
1/3 oz. peppermint schnapps
1/3 oz. Parfait Amour

Blue Jay

1/3 oz. Parfait Amour
1/3 oz. peppermint schnapps
1/3 oz. crème de banane

Blue Monday

1/3 oz. crème de banane
1/3 oz. Parfait Amour
1/3 oz. vodka

Boilermaker

1 oz. whiskey
1 beer
The original my-girl-just-left-me drink and the staple of old John Wayne movies. Simply shoot the whiskey; then drink the beer.

Bottle Cap

1/2 oz. Jägermeister
1/2 oz. root beer schnapps
Shake and strain into a shot glass.

Brain Hemorrhage

1/2 oz. peach schnapps
1/4 oz. Baileys
dash of grenadine
Pour peach schnapps, then slowly pour in Baileys followed by grenadine. Awesome visual!

Brave Bull
½ oz. Kahlúa
½ oz. tequila

Broken-Down Golf Cart
⅓ oz. vodka
⅓ oz. Amaretto
⅓ oz. melon liqueur
Shake and strain into a shot glass.

Bubble Gum
¼ oz. Kahlúa
¼ oz. crème de banane
¼ oz. Parfait Amour
¼ oz. Baileys
*See also **Bazooka Joe***

Buca Bear
½ oz. root beer schnapps
½ oz. sambuca
7UP
Pour liqueurs into a shot glass. Drop into a glass filled with 7UP.

Burt Reynolds
½ oz. spiced rum
½ oz. butter ripple schnapps
Shake and strain into a shot glass.

Butch Cassidy
½ oz. apricot brandy
½ oz. Grand Marnier

Candy Apple
½ oz. apple schnapps
½ oz. cinnamon schnapps
½ oz. apple juice
Pour into a 2 oz. shot glasss.

The trouble with getting a
life is making the payments.
Anonymous

Candy Cane
⅓ oz. grenadine
⅓ oz. green crème de menthe
⅓ oz. peppermint schnapps
"We wish you a merry Christmas ..."

66

Cement Mixer
1 oz. Baileys
shot of lime juice
*Pour Baileys into a shot glass
and layer with lime juice for
some curdling fun.*

Charlie's Angel
3/4 oz. Amaretto
1/4 oz. cream

Cherry Bomb
½ oz. cherry whiskey
½ oz. vodka
½ glass Red Bull
*Pour vodka and whiskey into a
shot glass. Drop shot into Red
Bull and drink.*

China White
1/3 oz. white crème de cacao
1/3 oz. Baileys
1/3 oz. cinnamon schnapps
garnish: dusting of cinnamon

Chocolate Banana
1/3 oz. Kahlúa
1/3 oz. crème de banane
1/3 oz. Baileys

Chocolate Chip
1/3 oz. Swiss chocolate almond
   liqueur
1/3 oz. Baileys
1/3 oz. peppermint schnapps

Chocolate Monkey
½ oz. crème de cacao
½ oz. crème de banane
milk
*Pour liqueurs into a shot glass.
Drop into a glass filled with
milk.*

Christmas Hug
1/3 oz. Parfait Amour
1/3 oz. cherry brandy
1/3 oz. Baileys

Cliff Hanger
1/3 oz. Kahlúa
1/3 oz. Baileys
1/3 oz. brandy
*Yet another modification
of the classic B-52.*

Coco Nuts
½ oz. Malibu rum
½ oz. Frangelico

Coffee Bean

⅓ oz. Kahlúa
⅓ oz. anisette
⅓ oz. Southern Comfort

Coma

⅓ oz. Kahlúa
⅓ oz. crème de banane
⅓ oz. anisette

Some people use triple sec instead of anisette. You decide.

Cough Drop

½ oz. peppermint schnapps
½ oz. Drambuie

It tastes bad ... but it works!

Cowboy Rooster Vacuum

½ oz. Baileys
½ oz. root beer schnapps

Thanks to Jim Bogart for this tasty gem—my second favorite shooter.

Crazy Banana

⅔ oz. crème de banane
⅓ oz. cherry whiskey
7UP
pineapple juice

Pour liqueurs into a shot glass. Drop into a glass filled with 7UP and pineapple juice.

Cream Soda Drop

⅕ oz. Amaretto
⅖ oz. crème de banane
⅖ oz. melon liqueur
cranberry juice
soda water

Drop the liqueur shot into a short glass of cranberry juice and soda. Enjoy. Special thanks to Doug "Dash" Lapierre for this wicked drop shot.

Cruise Missile

⅓ oz. Kahlúa
⅓ oz. Baileys
⅓ oz. Malibu rum

Don't miss our show!
Six beautiful dancing girls!
Five beautiful costumes!
London nightclub poster

Cupid

⅓ oz. grenadine
⅓ oz. white crème de menthe
⅓ oz. triple sec or Cointreau

Your boss would prefer that you use triple sec. It's cheaper.

DC-3

⅓ oz. Kahlúa
⅓ oz. anisette
⅓ oz. Baileys

68

Death by Chocolate
⅔ oz. crème de cacao
⅓ oz. Kahlúa
chocolate milk
Pour liqueurs into a shot glass.
Drop into a glass filled with
chocolate milk.

Deep T
⅓ oz. Kahlúa
⅓ oz. Baileys
⅓ oz. vodka

Depth Charge
1 oz. rye
1 glass lager
Drop the shot of rye into a pint
glass of lager.

Depth Charge Shooter
⅓ oz. Kahlúa
⅓ oz. Baileys
⅓ oz. peppermint schnapps

Dingbat
⅓ oz. dark rum
⅓ oz. Kahlúa
⅓ oz. cream

Dirty Dog
¼ oz. tequila
¼ oz. Galliano
¼ oz. Grand Marnier
¼ oz. ouzo or Pernod

DOA
⅓ oz. Parfait Amour
⅓ oz. anisette
⅓ oz. tequila

Double Jack
½ oz. Yukon Jack
½ oz. Jack Daniel's
It must be late if someone's
ordering this one.

Dr. Pepper
¾ glass beer
¼ glass cola
1 oz. Amaretto
Pour beer and cola into a pint
glass. Drop in the shot of
Amaretto and consume.

Earthquake
⅓ oz. gin
⅓ oz. rye
⅓ oz. Pernod

Electric Banana
½ oz. crème de banane
½ oz. tequila

Electric Popsicle
¼ oz. Parfait Amour
¼ oz. vodka
¼ oz. crème de banane

Fox Trot
1/3 oz. Kahlúa
1/3 oz. Baileys
1/3 oz. tequila

Freight Train
1/2 oz. Jack Daniel's
1/2 oz. Grand Marnier

1/4 oz. lime juice
7UP to fill
Some bartenders omit the crème de banane, but I like it. Try it both ways.

French Connection
1/2 oz. cognac
1/2 oz. triple sec
I've seen this one done with tequila and Amaretto, but that's more of a Mexican-Italian connection. I prefer this "Grand Marnier–like" concoction.

Eskimo Pie
1/3 oz. Kahlúa
1/3 oz. peppermint schnapps
1/3 oz. cream
Serve this one cold, just like the original.

Fruit Loop
1/3 oz. strawberry liqueur
1/3 oz. melon liqueur
1/3 oz. crème de banane
Have you ever noticed that many shooters are simply child-hood treats with an adult edge? Being a grown-up rocks!

52nd Avenue
1/3 oz. pear liqueur
1/3 oz. Baileys
1/3 oz. crème de banane

Flame Thrower
1/3 oz. white crème de cacao
1/3 oz. Bénédictine
1/3 oz. brandy
You can substitute 2/3 oz. B & B for the Bénédictine and brandy, if you happen to have a bottle.

Fruit Salad
1/3 oz. grenadine
1/3 oz. crème de banane
1/3 oz. melon liqueur

Gatorader
⅓ oz. crème de banane
⅓ oz. strawberry liqueur
⅓ oz. cherry brandy

Georgia Peach
½ oz. Southern Comfort
½ oz. peach schnapps
7UP
orange juice
*Pour liqueurs into a shot glass.
Drop into a glass filled with
7UP and orange juice.*

Ghostbuster
⅓ oz. Kahlúa
⅓ oz. Baileys
⅓ oz. Grand Marnier
1 oz. rye
4 oz. cola
*Build B-52—Kahlúa, Baileys,
GM—and drop into 2 oz. shot
glass with rye and coke. Down!*

Girl Scout Cookie
½ oz. peppermint schnapps
½ oz. Kahlúa
1 oz. cream
*I would buy a box of these bad
boys.*

Gladiator
½ oz. Amaretto
½ oz. Southern Comfort
orange juice
soda water
*Layer the liqueurs in a shot
glass, then drop into a highball
glass filled with orange juice and
soda. Consume.*

Golden Russian
⅓ oz. Kahlúa
⅓ oz. Amaretto
⅓ oz. cream

Grasshopper
⅓ oz. brown crème de cacao
⅓ oz. green crème de menthe
⅓ oz. cream

Green Emerald
⅓ oz. green crème de menthe
⅓ oz. triple sec
⅓ oz. Swiss chocolate almond
  liqueur

Green Hornet
⅓ oz. Amaretto
⅓ oz. melon liqueur
⅓ oz. peppermint schnapps

Grenade
1 oz. flavored vodka
1 oz. Jägermeister
½ pint glass Red Bull
*Pour shots and gently wedge shot
glasses in the pint glass, with
Jäger shot slightly higher (i.e.,
the pin). Pull the Jäger shot and
drink. The remaining vodka
shot falls into the Red Bull,
making the chaser.*

Guam Bomb
⅓ oz. Kahlúa
⅓ oz. Baileys
⅓ oz. coconut rum

Guts

¾ oz. sloe gin
¼ oz. Baileys
*Pour a slow, intestine-like
stream of Baileys into the sloe
gin. Get it?*

Harbor Light

⅓ oz. green crème de menthe
⅓ oz. strawberry liqueur
⅓ oz. Cointreau

Highland Sling

⅓ oz. Drambuie
⅓ oz. Baileys
⅓ oz. B & B
Save this one for James Joyce's birthday.

Honey Dripper

⅓ oz. Galliano
⅓ oz. triple sec
⅓ oz. Baileys

Horny Monkey

¼ oz. Kahlúa
¼ oz. green crème de menthe
¼ oz. crème de banane
¼ oz. Baileys

Hurricane

¼ oz. anisette
¼ oz. blue curaçao
¼ oz. tequila
¼ oz. cream
*Pour the ingredients freely to
achieve a hurricane-like mess.*

Iguana

⅓ oz. Kahlúa
⅓ oz. tequila
⅓ oz. vodka

IRA

⅓ oz. Baileys
⅓ oz. Irish Mist
⅓ oz. Irish whiskey

Irish Car Bomb

½ oz. Baileys
½ oz. Irish whiskey
½ pint Guinness
Pour the shot. Drop into Guinness. Consume.

Irish Monkey

1/3 oz. Kahlúa
1/3 oz. Baileys
1/3 oz. crème de banane

Some bartenders make this without crème de banane, but the "banane" makes the "monkey."

Island Gold

1/3 oz. Malibu rum
1/3 oz. crème de banane
1/3 oz. Baileys

Jack Frost

1/2 oz. peppermint schnapps
1/2 oz. Jack Daniel's
Coke

Pour liqueurs into a shot glass. Drop into a glass filled with Coke.

Jäger Bomb

1 oz. Jägermeister
1/2 glass Red Bull

Drop shot into Red Bull and consume.

Jamaican Flag

1/3 oz. green crème de menthe
1/3 oz. crème de banane
1/3 oz. black sambuca

Irie and one love.

Jell-O Shot

2 packages Jell-O
boiling water
1 cup vodka

Prepare Jell-O as per instructions, substituting vodka—or

other spirit—for cold water. Cool. Pour into shot glasses or creative molds. Experiment!

Jelly Bean—Black

1/3 oz. grenadine
1/3 oz. black sambuca
1/3 oz. tequila

Jelly Bean—Coconut

1/3 oz. grenadine
1/3 oz. Malibu rum
1/3 oz. tequila

Add a little ouzo if you like.

Jelly Bean—Green

1/3 oz. grenadine
1/3 oz. white crème de menthe
1/3 oz. tequila

Jelly Bean—Licorice

1/3 oz. grenadine
1/3 oz. sambuca
1/3 oz. Southern Comfort

Shake ingredients with ice and strain into a shot glass.

Jelly Bean—Miscellaneous

1/3 oz. grenadine
1/3 oz. your choice
1/3 oz. tequila

The middle liqueur sets the jelly bean's flavor and/or color.

Jelly Bean—Orange

1/3 oz. grenadine
1/3 oz. Grand Marnier
1/3 oz. tequila

Jelly Bean—Red

⅓ oz. grenadine
⅓ oz. Chambord Royale
⅓ oz. tequila

Jelly Bean—White

⅓ oz. grenadine
⅓ oz. anisette
⅓ oz. tequila
Add a little ouzo if you like.

Kahlúa Candy Cane

⅓ oz. Kahlúa
⅓ oz. peppermint schnapps
⅓ oz. cream

> Only Irish coffee provides in a single glass all four essential food groups: alcohol, caffeine, sugar and fat.
> Alex Levine

Kamikaze

¾ oz. vodka
¾ oz. triple sec
½ oz. lime cordial
(A 2 oz. shot glass is needed.)
Whenever I get an order for this shot, I remember Tom Cruise's poem atop the bar in the movie Cocktail. *If you haven't seen this movie, rent it tonight!*

KAT

⅓ oz. Kahlúa
⅓ oz. anisette
⅓ oz. tequila

Kicker

⅓ oz. Kahlúa
⅓ oz. Amaretto
⅓ oz. Grand Marnier

Ko-cane

⅓ oz. Kahlúa
⅓ oz. Amaretto
⅓ oz. tequila

Landslide

⅓ oz. Kahlúa
⅓ oz. crème de banane
⅓ oz. Baileys
Some bartenders substitute Amaretto for crème de banane.

Lemon Drop

1 oz. vodka
1 lemon wedge
sugar
It goes like this: (1) sugar the lemon wedge, (2) shoot the vodka and (3) bite the lemon.

Licorice Lix

¾ oz. sambuca
¼ oz. orange juice

74

Liquid Cocaine

½ oz. Jägermeister
½ oz. Goldschläger
Shake ingredients with ice and strain into a shot glass.

Lotto 649

Face the bar and choose the bottle
  6th from the left
  4th from the right
  9th from the left
Pour equal amounts of each spirit using the layering guide or simply shake them. I created this shot back in 1988 to keep things interesting, a sort of "shot du jour." I set up my bottles in a customer-friendly manner; however, the random nature of the 649 makes it a risky choice at most bars.

Mandatory

½ oz. Baileys
½ oz. peppermint schnapps
The name says it all. You must try one of these.

M & M

½ oz. Kahlúa
½ oz. Amaretto
This beauty definitely "melts in your mouth."

Margarita

¾ oz. tequila
¼ oz. triple sec
garnish: lime wedge
Salt the rim of the shot glass.

Matty's Revenge

1 oz. tequila
1 drop grenadine
7UP
lime juice
Pour the tequila and grenadine shot. Drop into a glass filled with 7UP and lime juice. Thanks, Craig!

Melon Ball

½ oz. vodka
¼ oz. melon liqueur
¼ oz. pineapple juice

Mexican Chiller

¾ oz. tequila
¼ oz. Clamato juice
1 drop Tabasco sauce

Mexican Flag

⅓ oz. grenadine
⅓ oz. green crème de menthe
⅓ oz. tequila

Mexican Snowshoe

½ oz. green crème de menthe
½ oz. tequila
It's just fine to use peppermint schnapps instead of green crème de menthe.

Miami Ice
½ oz. Kahlúa
½ oz. coconut rum

Mo Bookley
⅓ oz. Kahlúa
⅓ oz. peppermint schnapps
⅓ oz. Baileys

Model T
⅓ oz. Kahlúa
⅓ oz. crème de banane
⅓ oz. Baileys

Mountain Dew
½ oz. melon liqueur
½ oz. Amaretto
7UP
lime juice
Pour liqueurs into a shot glass.
Drop into a glass filled with
7UP and lime juice.

MX Missile
⅓ oz. Kahlúa
⅓ oz. Baileys
⅓ oz. coconut rum

Nicoloscar
1 oz. brandy
½ lemon slice
½ tsp. instant coffee
½ tsp. coarse sugar
Rub coffee on one half of the
lemon slice and sugar on the
other half. Bite the lemon, then
shoot the brandy. I've heard this
shot called "Nashkaliska" and
"Michaloshka."

Nut Cracker
⅓ oz. melon liqueur
⅓ oz. Frangelico
⅓ oz. Baileys

Nut House
½ oz. Amaretto
½ oz. Frangelico
Coke
milk
Pour liqueurs into a shot glass.
Drop into a glass filled with
Coke and milk. Pour the Coke
first or the mixture will foam.

Oblivion
⅓ oz. Baileys
⅓ oz. Irish Mist
⅓ oz. Irish whiskey

O Canada
½ oz. Chambord
½ oz. Baileys

Orange Blossom
⅓ oz. Amaretto
⅓ oz. Baileys
⅓ oz. triple sec

Paralyzer Drop Shot
½ oz. Kahlúa
½ oz. vodka
Coke
milk
Pour Kahlúa and vodka into a
shot glass. Drop into a glass
filled with Coke and milk. Pour
the Coke first or the mixture will
foam.

PCB

⅓ oz. peppermint schnapps
⅓ oz. Cointreau
⅓ oz. Baileys

Peppermint Patty

¾ oz. Kahlúa
¾ oz. peppermint schnapps
½ oz. cream
(A 2 oz. shot glass is needed.)

Peppermint Push

½ oz. peppermint schnapps
½ oz. vodka

Popsicle

⅓ oz. apricot brandy
⅓ oz. vodka
⅓ oz. cream

Porn Star

½ oz. Red Sour Puss
½ oz. blue curaçao
Shake and strain into a shot glass.

Pousse-Café 1

⅛ oz. grenadine
⅛ oz. Kahlúa
⅛ oz. green crème de menthe
⅛ oz. Parfait Amour
⅛ oz. crème de banane
⅛ oz. Amaretto
⅛ oz. Cointreau
⅛ oz. Galliano
Layer liqueurs atop one another, starting with grenadine and ending with Galliano.

Pousse-Café 2

⅕ oz. Kahlúa
⅕ oz. Chambord
⅕ oz. Tia Maria
⅕ oz. Galliano
⅕ oz. Amaretto

Pousse-Café 3

⅕ oz. Chambord
⅕ oz. Frangelico
⅕ oz. Goldschläger
⅕ oz. Jägermeister
⅕ oz. Southern Comfort

Pousse-Café 4

⅕ oz. grenadine
⅕ oz. Kahlúa
⅕ oz. Galliano
⅕ oz. Amaretto
⅕ oz. Malibu rum

Pousse-Café 5

¼ oz. Drambuie
¼ oz. Cointreau
¼ oz. Grand Marnier
¼ oz. Malibu rum

....
... remember the mighty
oak was once a nut like you.
    Bullwinkle Moose
....

Prairie Fire

1 oz. tequila
Tabasco sauce to taste
Marinate some jalapeños in the tequila ahead of time for a real blast. Remove the evidence before serving.

Puppy's Nose
²/₅ oz. Kahlúa
²/₅ oz. peppermint schnapps
¹/₅ oz. Baileys
Sounds harmless enough.

Purple Mambo
¹/₂ oz. Parfait Amour
¹/₂ oz. anisette

Quick Silver
¹/₃ oz. white crème de cacao
¹/₃ oz. peppermint schnapps
¹/₃ oz. tequila

Raider
¹/₃ oz. Drambuie
¹/₃ oz. Baileys
¹/₃ oz. Grand Marnier

Red Hot
1 oz. peppermint schnapps
Tabasco sauce to taste
*Remember those little heart-
shaped candies? Same thing—
just better. See also **Prairie Fire***

Reese's Cup
²/₃ oz. white crème de cacao
¹/₃ oz. Baileys
1 peanut (unsalted)
*Drop a peanut into the shot
glass. Layer the liqueurs atop it.
Be sure to warn the recipient of
the peanut, or prepare to perform
the Heimlich maneuver.*

Rigor Mortis
¹/₃ oz. Kahlúa
¹/₃ oz. Baileys
¹/₃ oz. bourbon

There is nothing wrong with
sobriety in moderation.
  John Ciardi

Rush Hour
¹/₃ oz. Kahlúa
¹/₃ oz. sambuca
¹/₃ oz. Baileys

Russian Roulette

¹/₃ oz. vodka
¹/₃ oz. Galliano
¹/₄ oz. sambuca
sugared orange round

Pour the vodka and Galliano into a shot glass. Pour the sambuca into a snifter and light. Then slowly pour the flaming sambuca into the shot glass, extinguish and consume. Bite the sugared orange. Thanks to Naomie Theriault!

Ryan's Rush

¹/₃ oz. Kahlúa
¹/₃ oz. Baileys
¹/₃ oz. white rum

Sambuca Shot

1 oz. sambuca
3 coffee beans

Float the beans atop the sambuca. Ideally, this shot is served flaming, but be very careful, as the light-blue flame is difficult to see and flaming sambuca is akin to napalm.

Sangrita (makes 4)

2 oz. tomato juice
²/₃ oz. orange juice
¹/₃ oz. lime juice
¹/₃ oz. grenadine
dash of Tabasco sauce
coarse salt and pepper
shots of tequila

Shake the first five ingredients with ice. Rim four shot glasses with salt and pepper and fill with strained mixture. Serve with four shots of tequila.

Scooby Snack Shot

¹/₅ oz. coconut rum
¹/₅ oz. crème de banane
¹/₅ oz. melon liqueur
¹/₅ oz. pineapple juice
¹/₅ oz. cream

Shake ingredients with ice and strain into a shot glass.

Screaming Green Lizard

¹/₂ oz. tequila
¹/₂ oz. Chartreuse

I can't think of a better use for that dusty bottle of Chartreuse. Can you?

Screwdriver, Cordless

³/₄ oz. vodka
¹/₄ oz. Cointreau
1 orange wedge
sugar

It goes like this: (1) sugar the orange wedge, (2) pour and shoot the vodka and Cointreau and (3) bite the orange.

747

¹/₃ oz. Kahlúa
¹/₃ oz. Amaretto
¹/₃ oz. Baileys

Sicilian Kiss

¹/₂ oz. Amaretto
¹/₂ oz. Southern Comfort

Silver Bullet 1

¹/₃ oz. anisette
¹/₃ oz. brown crème de cacao
¹/₃ oz. Baileys
You don't like this version? Try the next one.

Silver Bullet 2

¹/₂ oz. green crème de menthe
¹/₂ oz. tequila

Silver Thread

¹/₃ oz. crème de banane
¹/₃ oz. peppermint schnapps
¹/₃ oz. Baileys

Skittles

¹/₂ oz. butter ripple schnapps
¹/₂ oz. lime juice

Slippery Chicken

¹/₃ oz. crème de banane
¹/₃ oz. Amaretto
¹/₃ oz. Baileys
Funny name. Tasty shooter.

Slippery Nipple

¹/₂ oz. sambuca
¹/₂ oz. Baileys
Layer Baileys atop sambuca. Enjoy!

Snake Bite

⁴/₅ oz. Yukon Jack
¹/₅ oz. lime juice

Snowshoe

¹/₂ oz. peppermint schnapps
¹/₂ oz. tequila
Some bartenders use white crème de cacao rather than schnapps. Bartenders rarely agree.

Space Case

¹/₃ oz. Kahlúa
¹/₃ oz. crème de banane
¹/₃ oz. Grand Marnier

Spider Bite

¹/₂ oz. anisette
¹/₂ oz. tequila

Stars and Stripes

¹/₃ oz. Chambord
¹/₃ oz. Parfait Amour
¹/₃ oz. sambuca
"Oh say, does that star-spangled banner yet wave..."

Stiletto

¹/₃ oz. Kahlúa
¹/₃ oz. peppermint schnapps
¹/₃ oz. Grand Marnier

Stinger

½ oz. white crème de menthe
½ oz. brandy

Storm Warning

⅓ oz. brown crème de cacao
⅓ oz. cherry brandy
⅓ oz. Baileys

Strawberry Blonde

⅓ oz. strawberry liqueur
⅓ oz. white crème de cacao
⅓ oz. Baileys

Strawberry Shake

½ oz. Baileys
½ oz. strawberry liqueur
*Top with whipped cream to
make a Strawberry Shortcake.*

Sunscreen

½ oz. Malibu rum
½ oz. crème de banane
pineapple juice
*Pour spirits into a shot glass.
Drop into a glass filled with
pineapple juice.*

Surf's Up

⅓ oz. blue curaçao
⅓ oz. Malibu rum
⅓ oz. Baileys

Sweet Peach

⅓ oz. Amaretto
⅓ oz. peach schnapps
⅓ oz. orange juice

T & T

⅓ oz. Amaretto
⅓ oz. Baileys
⅓ oz. Grand Marnier

Tartan Special

⅓ oz. Glayva
⅓ oz. Drambuie
⅓ oz. Baileys

It takes a big man to cry,
but it takes a bigger man
to laugh at that man.
   Jack Handey,
"Saturday Night Live"

I drink when I have
occasion, and sometimes
when I have no occasion.
   Miguel de Cervantes

Tequila Fizz / Drop / Puff
1 oz. tequila
7UP
Drop the tequila into the 7UP and enjoy.

Tequila Shot
1 oz. tequila
1 lime wedge
1 pinch salt
This is the accepted method for shooting tequila: (1) moisten the web between your thumb and first finger, (2) salt it, (3) lick the salt, (4) drink the tequila, (5) bite the lime wedge and, finally, (5) flinch.

Tequila Slammer
1 oz. tequila
1 oz. ginger ale
Pour into a shot glass. Cover glass with palm. Slam on bar, then drink while fizzing.

Test Tube Baby
½ oz. tequila
½ oz. Amaretto
1 drop Baileys
Pour the first two ingredients. Slowly drop in the Baileys.

Tetanus Shot
½ oz. Drambuie
½ oz. Jack Daniel's

The Titanic
⅓ oz. Kahlúa
⅓ oz. Amaretto
⅓ oz. Baileys
If you'll pardon the pun, this one goes down quickly.

TKO
⅓ oz. tequila
⅓ oz. Kahlúa
⅓ oz. ouzo

Tooti-Fruiti
⅓ oz. crème de banane
⅓ oz. cherry brandy
⅓ oz. pear brandy

Tootsie Roll
⅓ oz. brown crème de cacao
⅓ oz. Kahlúa
⅓ oz. orange juice

Liquor is not a necessity.
It is a means of momentarily
side-stepping necessity.
  Clifton Fadiman

Traffic Light
⅓ oz. Chambord
⅓ oz. green crème de menthe
⅓ oz. crème de banane
Galliano also works for the yellow layer, as does grenadine for the red.

Volcano
⅓ oz. grenadine
⅓ oz. tequila
⅓ oz. Pernod

Watermelon

½ oz. Southern
  Comfort
½ oz. melon liqueur
Serve this one very cold.

Waterslide

½ oz. Parfait Amour
½ oz. anisette

Willpower

½ oz. Jägermeister
½ oz. root beer schnapps
beer
*Pour liqueurs into a shot
glass. Drop into a pint glass
half filled with lager or ale.
Thanks, Will!*

Windex Drop Shot

1 oz. blue curaçao
7UP
*Invert an empty glass over
the shot. Flip so that the
curaçao shot is upside down.
Fill the glass with 7UP.
Practice makes perfect!*

Windex Shooter

⅘ oz. vodka
⅕ oz. Parfait Amour

Work is a fine thing if it
doesn't take too much of
your spare time.
  Anonymous

Zipper

⅓ oz. crème de banane
⅓ oz. peppermint schnapps
⅓ oz. Baileys

I don't want to belong
to any club that will
accept me as a member.
  Groucho Marx

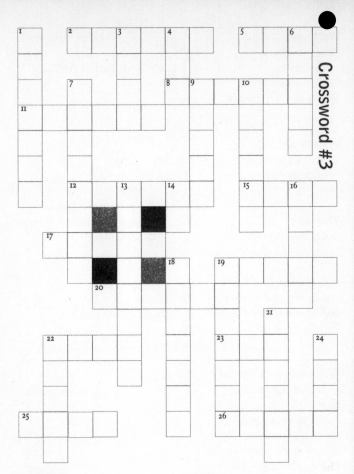

ACROSS

2. China White garnish
5. cognac classification
8. martini with an onion
11. shake & _ _ _ _ _ _
12. distilled wine
15. bourbon's grain
17. Kramer's smoke
19. Bond's martini
20. Greek brandy
22. Caesar's rimmer
23. where drinks are made
25. Japanese rice wine
26. tequila's plant

DOWN

1. Irish or Scotch
3. imbiber's ride
6. pony measure
7. Scotch & heather honey liqueur
9. Chianti's homeland
10. single malt?
13. almond-flavored liqueur
14. crème _ _ menthe
16. on the _ _ _ _ _
18. Irish cream liqueur
19. Italian licorice liqueur
21. almond syrup
22. drinking tube
24. red or white

solution p. 135

84

GARNISHES

A well-chosen garnish enhances the flavor and appearance of a martini. But for the past several decades, bartenders have relied on the celery stick, maraschino cherry, lemon, lime, orange and pimento-stuffed green olive as their sole sources of inspiration.

The renaissance of the martini culture, however, has put greater demands and expectations on the professional bartender, or at least those who attain the status of "Bar Chef" at the highest levels. Let's go back in time for a moment. The 1950s and '60s brought about the tiki style of cocktails, which included the mai tai, zombie, piña colada, daiquiri and other well-dressed, spirited refreshments. These tasty concoctions were decorated with campy, ornate garnishes and showcased in flamboyant (often gaudy) glassware.

A mai tai is an imposter at best until it's presented in a glass shaped like a bamboo stalk, garnished with a skewered orange slice, cherry and pineapple wedge, and decorated with an Asian parasol and a hula-dancer-shaped swizzle stick. Then it's just plain fun. Presentation is everything. Think about it: when dining out, we would be totally unimpressed if our server presented our meal without appropriate plating and garnish. We have every right to feel the same way about our martinis.

So get creative and have some fun with your garnishes. There are so many available options, and part of the fun is choosing the one that is just right for the drink you're creating. The following is meant not to overwhelm, but rather to inspire a brainstorming session of your own. If it's edible, it's a garnish looking for a recipe.

Fruits

Citrus fruits are versatile—the workhorse of the cocktail industry—as they provide wedges, circles, slices, twists, zest and juice. But the fruit category has so much more to offer. A single raspberry, a slice of shockingly green kiwi or a piece of star fruit can be the perfect final touch to your martini masterpiece. Martini artists can use fruit to inject color, shape and flavor into their designs, so here's a list to get you started: lemons, limes, tangerines, oranges, grapefruits, apples, pineapples, kiwis, star fruits, papayas, coconuts, strawberries, raspberries (any kind of berry, really), grapes, watermelons, cantaloupes, honeydew melons, crab apples, bananas, prunes, cherries, capers (yes, they're fruit) and olives (ditto).

To make a twist, cut the outermost colorful rind of citrus fruit into strips, avoiding the underlying bitter, usually white, pith. Cutting a thin slice through the equator of the fruit will yield a membrane-spoked wheel, which can be sliced once more from edge to center and placed elegantly on the rim of a glass. Slice a spherical fruit from end to end into fourths or eighths to create wedges. Whenever possible, replace processed orange, lemon or lime juices with freshly squeezed. Melons can be served as balls, wedges or slices. Smaller fruits, such as berries, grapes, prunes, capers, etc., are ready to go (after a thorough washing). Dried fruit can be shredded, sliced into thin strips or chopped into wedges or cubes.

The olive: you have many options when using the ubiquitous olive as a garnish. First of all, there are many varieties to choose from, including the tart Alphonso, salty Kalamata, juicy Hondroelia, bitter Moroccan, or the standard pimento-stuffed Spanish Manzanilla and Italian Sicilian olives. (Whichever you choose, olives must be pitted to protect the imbiber's teeth.) Use them plain or stuffed with any of a variety of fillings: the aforementioned pimento, garlic, peppers or even blue cheese.

Vegetables

Although the popular Caesar is well known for its celery stalk, other vegetables are often overlooked as potential sources of garnishes. Don't forget that the garnish is usually eaten, so it must be fresh and flavorful, with a pleasing appearance. Here are a few vegetable ideas: celery, cherry tomatoes, sweet and hot peppers, onions, carrots, cucumbers, asparagus, green onions, okra, radishes, pickles, green beans and artichokes. Celery, carrots, green onion and asparagus should be cut into stalks or sticks. Dense or whole vegetables, such as cherry tomatoes and radishes, are best served washed and uncut.

Cucumbers produce wheels, wedges and rinds (much like citrus fruit), while hollow vegetables, like sweet peppers, are best served sliced into thin, curled garnishes. Vegetable garnishes are best suited to drinks containing tequila or vodka, mixed with vegetable juices and a dash of Tabasco sauce. Experimentation is key. For example, the Sangrita—which contains tequila, lime and tomato juices—can "get by" garnished with a simple wedge of lime. Add thin slices of flavorful red, yellow and green peppers, then finish with a fresh stalk of green onion, and the ordinary becomes extraordinary.

Herbs, Spices and Flavorings

Herbs and spices are an underutilized source of garnish, which is particularly odd, given that they are common ingredients in spirits and liqueurs. I direct you once again to the classic Caesar, whose character is defined by the judicious use of spices—Tabasco sauce, Worcestershire sauce, salt and pepper. So don't be afraid to experiment with the following: cinnamon, cloves, ginger, nutmeg, star anise, sugar (brown, white, crystal and cane), coffee, mint, basil, oregano, tarragon, rosemary, cumin, coriander, salt (rock, sea and kosher) and pepper (black and white).

Many of these can be used in a variety of forms. Dried spices and seeds—cinnamon sticks and star anise, for example—are nature-made, ready-to-introduce garnishes. The fresh, soft, unblemished stalks and leaves of herbs add natural flavor, visual appeal and fragrance to recipes. Ground spices, and flavorings such as cane sugar or coffee, when shaken firmly with ice, add rich flavors or sweetness—or both. The possibilities are endless. Replace the standard martini's olive garnish with fresh basil or tarragon leaves. Dust a Velvet Hammer (or any cream-based martini) with ginger, cloves or nutmeg for a unique presentation and taste. For a recipe that could use a little extra sweetness, rim the edge of the glass with brown or crystal sugar. And don't forget that spice garnishing is a complex art: too little confuses the palate, while too much overwhelms it. Fresh ingredients and practice make perfect.

Edible Flowers

Edible flowers are flavorful, fragrant and pleasing to the eye and, thus, make excellent garnishes. A few recommendations: angelica, apple blossoms, carnations, chamomile, chrysanthemums, citrus blossoms, dandelions, elderberries, fuchsia, hibiscus, honeysuckle, hyacinth, jasmine, lavender, marigolds, petunias, primroses, roses and sage blossoms.

Check with a florist, chef or botanist for additional choices (and beware of non-edible varieties). Flowers may be presented whole or in petals, but must always be in natural, colorful, pristine condition—without blemishes. The pale pink apple blossom is a perfect match for the Blue Martini, while a bright red hyacinth makes a stunning addition to the creamy Pink Lady. As always, experiment, keeping the essence of the particular martini in mind, and you'll never go wrong.

Candy

There's no denying it: candy makes everyone happy. Why not spread some of that joy around? Here's a list to get you started: chocolate (bar, powder, flakes and melted), mini marshmallows, Smarties, M&M's, Hershey's Kisses, Life Savers, lollipops, crushed candy bars and caramels. Hard, coated or floatable candies that remain intact after minutes of submersion are simple drop-in garnishes. Chocolate may be heated and then drizzled into a chilled martini glass to harden before the alcohol is added. Chocolate flakes or broken candy may be sprinkled on top once you've made the martini, adding sweetness and flavor.

Seafood

A spicy, full-bodied martini is the perfect candidate for seafood garnish: shrimp, scallops, crab or lobster. Why not sauté jumbo shrimp in Pernod, then cool before adding to a Caesar? Or place a sautéed scallop on the rim of the glass like you would a lime wedge? Of course, seafood must be absolutely fresh and kept well chilled until the very moment it becomes garnish.

Sauces

Sauces are shaken with ingredients—firmly—and strained into the martini glass. You'll have to experiment to figure out how much of which condiment should be added. This list is just a starting point: Tabasco sauce, Worcestershire sauce, Louisiana Hot Sauce, mustard, curry and horseradish. It's up to you where you go from here.

And a note for bartenders: make sure that all bottles and containers that store ingredients are completely clean, with intact labels.

Style

The martini is all about style. The garnish may be the finishing touch on a work of art, but don't forget that presentation is affected by not only the obvious elements such as glassware and garnish, but also seemingly small factors such as straws, coasters, napkins, room lighting, music and the general atmosphere. Remember, expectations are high. Browse your local hobby, housewares and thrift stores for inspiration. Walk the produce aisle, looking beyond your usual choices. Sit down with a piece of fruit and whittle away. And don't forget to reward yourself for all this hard work with a well-chilled, well-garnished martini.

QUOTES

" . . . your body is not a temple, it's an amusement park.
Enjoy the ride."
—Anthony Bourdain

"Always do sober what you said you'd do drunk.
That will teach you to keep your mouth shut."
—Ernest Hemingway

"Beer is the cause and solution to all of life's problems."
—Homer Simpson

Brian: "You're drunk."
Stewie: "You're sexy."
"Family Guy"

"Dost thou think, because thou art virtuous,
there shall be no more cakes and ale?"
—Sir Toby Belch ("Twelfth Night," William Shakespeare)

"A man hath no better thing under the sun,
than to eat, and to drink, and to be merry."
—Ecclesiastes 8:15

"I never have more than one drink before dinner.
But I do like that one to be large and very strong
and very cold and very well made."
—James Bond (*Casino Royale*, Ian Fleming)

"I see you're drinking one percent.
Is that 'cause you think you're fat?
'Cause you're not. You could be drinking
whole if you wanted to."
—Napoleon Dynamite (*Napoleon Dynamite*)

"Bring in the bottled lightning,
a clean tumbler, and a corkscrew."
—Charles Dickens (*The Life and Adventures of Nicholas
Nickleby*)

"I don't have a girlfriend. But I do know a
woman who'd be mad at me for saying that."
—Mitch Hedberg

"I play a position where you make mistakes. The only people
who don't make them at a hockey game are the ones watching."
—Patrick Roy

"Some people skate to the puck. I skate to
where the puck is going to be. You miss one
hundred percent of the shots you never take."
—Wayne Gretzky

"Biologically, I'm ten. Chronologically, I'm thirty-three.
In hockey years, I'm sixty-six."
—Mark Messier

"Forget about style. Worry about results."
—Bobby Orr

"Winning does solve everything."
—Joe Sakic

MULLIGAN'S INTRODUCTION TO CIGARS

Cigar production contains many similarities to that of fine wine and cognac. Tobacco seeds are carefully selected, grown and harvested, then fermented and aged. And like a fine wine, a choice cigar isn't simply manufactured; it is constructed, often by the hands of a talented craftsman.

Currently, over 650 brands are available, with qualities ranging from inferior to sublime. The following is a general introduction to the care and enjoyment of the cigar.

Classification

A cigar's outer wrapper is classified by six basic shades:

- Double claro: light green to tan
- Claro: light tan to pale green
- Natural: light brown to brown
- Colorado: brown to reddish-brown
- Maduro: dark red to brown
- Oscuro: dark brown
- Candela: green

Length and diameter classify cigar shapes. Length is given in inches and diameter in ring gauges (RG). One ring gauge is $\frac{1}{64}$th of an inch, so a 32 RG cigar has a diameter of one-half inch. Cigars are further classified as parejos (straight-sided) or figurados (irregular-shaped). It is important to note that different manufacturers may follow their own classification scheme.

Common parejos:

Corona:	$5\frac{1}{2}" - 6" \times 42$RG
Double corona:	$6\frac{1}{2}" - 7" \times 49 - 52$RG
Churchill:	$7" \times 47 - 48$RG
Robustos:	$5" - 5\frac{1}{2}" \times 50$RG
Panetelas:	$7" \times 38$RG
Lonsdale:	$6" - 6\frac{1}{4}" \times 42 - 44$RG

Common figurados:

- Pyramid: pointed head (the end you smoke) widening to an open foot (the end you light)
- Torpedo: pointed head with a bulging center
- Perfecto: rounded ends with a bulging center (the kind that blow up in cartoons)
- Culebras: 3 panetelas braided together (you unbraid and smoke them one at a time)
- Diademas: A huge pyramid-shaped cigar, measuring up to 8 inches

Care and Storage

Cigars are best stored at a humidity of 70% within a temperature range of 65°F–70°F. Proper storage is critical in order to maintain the structural integrity and taste of the cigar. A well-crafted cigar deserves this respect.

Cigars are often enclosed in tubos (glass, wood or aluminum tubes), an amatista (a jar of fifty), boxes of twenty-five or a humidor, a humid and often decorative display case.

Preparation and Smoking

Examine the cigar, noting color, scent, texture and feel. Soft or hard spots may indicate uneven filler, which could affect flavor and smooth burning. Blemishes or cracks might be signs of improper storage or repeated cycles of rapid drying and hydration. Conversely, a moist, firmly packed cigar with an oily sheen is a good thing, suggesting a positive experience will follow.

Before lighting the cigar, its protective cap or "flag" must be cut. This process is called "clipping," and there are three preferred clipping methods:

- the pierce—pierce the tip with several holes
- the straight or guillotine cut—snip off the cap, exposing the maximum surface area to flame
- the V-cut or cat's eye—minimizes damage to the foot

The method you choose is a matter of personal preference, though the straight cut is the most popular choice.

Next comes lighting. Butane is a good fuel choice, as it is odorless and tasteless. Matches are also fine, but allow the sulfur to burn from the match before introducing it to the cigar. Hold a flame one-half inch from the foot of the cigar, warming the tip for a few seconds. Then, ignite the cigar with gentle puffs until the tip is uniformly glowing. A firm white or light-gray ash is the sign of a good cigar, indicating quality construction and tobaccos.

There's no need to inhale, as the tongue, palate and nose receive a cigar's taste and character. Simply puff slowly every few minutes, rotating the cigar for even burning. Look for the presence of smooth, woody, sweet, spicy or peppery nuances. Notice the finish, how it lingers on the palate. A 6" × 42RG corona should offer about half an hour of smoking, while larger robustos can last significantly longer.

On your next trip to the pub, try something different. May I suggest a vintage port or single-malt Scotch accompanied by your skillful choice of a fine cigar.

Thanks to Sean "Ghostly" Lyttle for his views. For more information contact your local tobacconist or investigate these Internet sites:

www.cigaraficionado.com
www.cigarweekly.com
www.cigarwoman.com

1000 REASONS TO PARTY

January 01
New Year's/Hangover Day
1969 Verne "Minnie Me" Troyer
1968 John Paul Tremblay
1919 J.D. Salinger

January 02
Ancestry Day (Haiti)
1983 Kate Bosworth
1934 First US liquor store opens
1920 Isaac Asimov

January 03
1969 Michael Schumacher
1956 Mel Gibson
1939 Bobby Hull
1892 J.R.R. Tolkien

January 04
1976 Gabriel Aubry
1963 Dave Foley
1809 Louis Braille
1643 Sir Isaac Newton

January 05
National Bird Day (US)
1969 Marilyn Manson
1948 Ted Lange
1931 Robert Duvall

January 06
Little Christmas (Ireland)
1982 Tiffany "New York" Pollard
1955 Rowan Atkinson
1412 Joan of Arc

January 07
Distaff Day—Pranks (Europe)
1964 Nicolas Cage
1957 Katie Couric
1800 Millard Filmore

January 08
1967 R. Kelly
1948 David Bowie
1942 Stephen Hawking
1935 Elvis Presley

January 09
1982 Kate Middleton
1944 Jimmy Page
1935 Bob Denver
1913 Richard Nixon

January 10
1953 Pat Benatar
1949 George Foreman
1945 Rod Stewart
1938 Frank Mahovlich

January 11
1971 Mary J. Blige
1946 Naomi Judd
1934 Jean Chrétien
1815 Sir John A. Macdonald

January 12
1966 Batman premieres
1955 Kirstie Alley
1954 Howard Stern
1944 Joe Frasier

January 13
St. Knut's Day
    (Sweden/Finland)
1977 Orlando Bloom
1966 Patrick Dempsey
1961 Julia Louis-Dreyfus

January 14
1969 Jason Bateman
1968 LL Cool J
1874 Albert Schweitzer
1741 Benedict Arnold

January 15
1951 Charo
1929 Martin Luther King, Jr.
1926 Chuck Berry
1907 Dr. Lee De Forest
    patents the vacuum tube

January 16
Nat'l Religious Freedom Day
1979 Aaliyah
1974 Kate Moss
1959 Sade

January 17
1942 Muhammad Ali
1929 Jacques Plante
1899 Al Capone
1706 Benjamin Franklin

January 18
1965 Dave Attell
1955 Kevin Costner
1904 Cary Grant
1892 Oliver Hardy

January 19
1971 Shawn Wayans
1946 Dolly Parton
1943 Janis Joplin
1809 Edgar Allan Poe

January 20
1966 Rainn Wilson
1956 Bill Maher
1952 Paul Stanley
1942 Phil Esposito

January 21
National Hug Day (US)
1941 Placido Domingo
1925 Benny Hill
1824 Thomas Jonathan
    "Stonewall" Jackson

January 22
1965 D.J. Jazzy Jeff
1957 Mike Bossy
1948 George Foreman
1935 Sam Cooke

January 23

1986 The Rock and Roll Hall of Fame inducts its first members (Buddy Holly, Chuck Berry and Ray Charles, among others)
1974 Tiffani-Amber Thiessen
1969 Brendon Shanahan
1832 Édouard Manet

January 24

1968 Will Smith
1949 John Belushi
1941 Neil Diamond
1935 Beer is sold in cans for the first time

January 25

Burns Night (Scotland)
1981 Alicia Keys
1882 Virginia Woolf
1874 W. Somerset Maugham

January 26

1961 Wayne Gretzky
1955 Eddie Van Halen
1925 Paul Newman
1788 First fleet of British convicts arrive at Sydney Cove

January 27

1948 Mikhail Baryshnikov
1880 Edison patents the incandescent lamp
1832 Lewis Carroll
1756 Wolfgang Mozart

January 28

1981 Elijah Wood
1968 Sarah McLachlan
1912 Jackson Pollock
1822 Alexander Mackenzie

January 29

1988 Canadian Ben Johnson breaks his own fifty-yard dash world record at 5.15 seconds
1954 Oprah Winfrey
1945 Tom Selleck
1879 W.C. Fields

January 30

1974 Christian Bale
1951 Phil Collins
1930 Gene Hackman
1882 Franklin Delano Roosevelt

January 31

1981 Justin Timberlake
1971 Minnie Driver
1947 Nolan Ryan
1923 Carol Channing

February 01

Black History Month begins
1948 Rick James
1901 Clark Gable
1882 Louis St. Laurent

February 02

Groundhog Day
1975 Drew Barrymore
1953 Duane "Dog" Chapman
1905 Ayn Rand
1882 James Joyce

February 03
Heroes' Day (Mozambique)
1907 James A. Michener
1894 Norman Rockwell
1500 Johannes Gutenberg

February 04
1973 Oscar De La Hoya
1959 Lawrence Taylor
1948 Alice Cooper
1913 Rosa Parks

February 05
1948 Christopher Guest
1936 National Wildlife Federation forms
1934 Hank Aaron
1914 William S. Burroughs

February 06
1962 Axl Rose
1945 Bob Marley
1919 Zsa Zsa Gabor
1895 Babe Ruth

February 07
1966 Chris Rock
1964 The Beatles arrive in America
1962 Garth Brooks
1812 Charles Dickens

February 08
Nirvana Day (Buddhism)
1974 Seth Green
1931 James Dean
1828 Jules Verne

February 09
1963 Travis Tritt
1944 Alice Walker
1943 Joe Pesci
1909 Carmen Miranda

February 10
2005 Largest portion of noodles is served in Indonesia (9,197 lbs)
1989 Ron Brown is elected as the first black chairman of a major US party
1940 Roberta Flack
1893 Jimmy Durante

February 11
1957 NHL Players Association forms in New York City
1936 Burt Reynolds
1926 Leslie Nielsen
1847 Thomas Edison

February 12
Darwin Day (International)
2001 First asteroid landing
1955 Arsenio Hall
1809 Abraham Lincoln

February 13
1950 Peter Gabriel
1944 Jerry Springer
1942 Peter Tork
1923 Chuck Yeager

February 14
Valentine's Day

Singles Awareness Day
1934 Florence Henderson
1913 Jimmy Hoffa

February 15
Parinirvana Day (Buddhism)
1964 Canada adopts the maple
    leaf flag
1954 Matt Groening
1564 Galileo Galilei

February 16
1964 The Beatles' second
    appearance on "The
    Ed Sullivan Show"
1959 John McEnroe
1958 Ice-T
1940 Sonny Bono

February 17
1981 Paris Hilton
1972 Denise Richards
1963 Michael Jordan
1962 Lou Diamond Phillips

February 18
1965 Dr. Dre
1957 Vanna White
1954 John Travolta
1930 Pluto is discovered

February 19
2004 Largest portion of
    fries is served (812.4 lbs,
    United Kingdom)
1963 Seal
1940 Smokey Robinson
1473 Nicolaus Copernicus

February 20
1967 Kurt Cobain
1963 Charles Barkley
1942 Phil Esposito
1927 Sidney Poitier

February 21
Mother Language Day
1943 David Geffen
1933 Nina Simone
1931 Alka Seltzer is
    introduced

February 22
1962 Steve "Crocodile Hunter"
    Irwin
1959 First Daytona 500
    auto race
1810 Frédéric Chopin
1732 George Washington

February 23
1949 Marc Garneau
1944 Johnny Winter
1910 First radio contest held
    (Philadelphia)
1868 W.E.B. Du Bois

February 24
National Artist Day
    (Thailand)
1955 Steve Jobs
1950 George Thorogood
1921 Abe Vigoda

February 25
People Power Day
    (Philippines)
1943 George Harrison

1909 Zeppo Marx
1841 Pierre-Auguste Renoir

February 26

1932 Johnny Cash
1928 Fats Domino
1916 Jackie Gleason
1829 Levi Strauss

February 27

1981 Josh Grobin
1967 Pink Floyd release their
first single, "Arnold Layne"
1932 Elizabeth Taylor
1902 John Steinbeck

February 28

1973 Eric Lindros
1955 Gilbert Gottfried
1940 First televised basketball
game (New York City)
1901 Linus Pauling

February 29

1980 Gordie Howe,
800th goal
1976 Jeff "Ja Rule" Atkins
1960 Tony Robbins
1960 First Playboy club opens
(Chicago)

March 01

Heroes' Day (Paraguay)
1994 Justin Bieber
1954 Ron Howard
1927 Harry Belafonte

March 02

1962 Jon Bon Jovi
1944 Lou Reed
1931 Mikhail Gorbachev
1904 Dr. Seuss

March 03

Hinamatsuri ("Girl's Day,"
Japan)
1962 Herschel Walker
1923 First "TIME" magazine
published
1847 Alexander Graham Bell

March 04

1963 Jason Curtis Newsted
1954 Catherine O'Hara
1936 First flight of the
Hindenburg airship (Germany)
1678 Antonio Vivaldi

March 05

1975 Niki Taylor
1974 Eva Mendes
1958 Andy Gibb
1955 Penn Jillette

March 06

1972 Shaquille O'Neal
1906 Lou Costello
1619 Cyrano De Bergerac
1475 Michelangelo

March 07

1964 Wanda Sykes
1942 Tammy Faye Baker
1876 Alexander Graham Bell
patents the telephone
1872 Piet Mondrian

March 08
International Women's Day
1976 Freddie Prinze, Jr.
1972 First flight of the
    Goodyear blimp
1945 Mickey Dolenz

March 09
1976 Ben Mulroney
1971 Emmanuel Lewis
1961 Soviets launch a dog into
    space
1934 Yuri Gagarin

March 10
1963 Rick Rubin
1958 Sharon Stone
1953 Paul Haggis
1940 Chuck Norris

March 11
Youth Day (Zambia)
1952 Douglas Adams
1950 Bobby McFerrin
1931 Rupert Murdoch

March 12
1978 Bobby Hull scores his
    1000th goal
1946 Liza Minnelli
1922 Jack Kerouac
1821 Sir John Abbott

March 13
1950 Williams H. Macy
1914 W.O. Mitchell
1911 L. Rob Hubbard
1855 Percival Lowell

March 14
1947 Billy Crystal
1933 Michael Caine
1933 Quincy Jones
1879 Albert Einstein

March 15
World Consumer Rights Day
1975 Will.i.am
1961 Fabio
1767 Andrew Jackson

March 16
1968 General Motors produces
    its 100 millionth automo-
    bile
1961 Todd McFarlane
1949 Erik Estrada
1926 Jerry Lewis

March 17
Saint Patrick's Day
1967 Billy Corgan
1951 Kurt Russell
1919 Nat "King" Cole

March 18
1972 Dane Cook
1970 Queen Latifah
1893 Lord Stanley pledges to
    donate a silver challenge
    cup to the best hockey team
    in Canada
1496 Mary Tudor

March 19
Mojoday (Discordianism)
1955 Bruce Willis

1947 Glenn Close
1848 Wyatt Earp

1942 Aretha Franklin
1807 The slave trade is abolished in the British Empire

March 20
1957 Spike Lee
1948 Bobby Orr
1939 Brian Mulroney
1928 Fred "Mr." Rogers

March 26
1950 Martin Short
1948 Steven Tyler
1944 Diana Ross
1931 Leonard Nimoy

March 21
Harmony Day (Australia)
1962 Matthew Broderick
1962 Rosie O'Donell
1685 Johann Sebastian Bach

March 27
World Theatre Day
1998 Viagra is approved by the US FDA
1970 Mariah Carey
1963 Quentin Tarantino

March 22
1972 Elvis Stojko
1948 Andrew Lloyd Webber
1943 George Benson
1931 William Shatner

March 28
1986 Lady Gaga
1970 Vince Vaughn
1954 Reba McEntire
1868 Maxim Gorky

March 23
1968 Damon Albarn
1953 Chaka Khan
1905 Joan Crawford
1857 Elisha Otis' first elevator is installed (New York City)

March 29
1964 Elle McPherson
1943 Eric Idle
1886 First batch of Coca-Cola brewed in Dr. John Pemberton's backyard (USA)
1867 Cy Young

March 24
1962 The Undertaker (WWE professional wrestler)
1936 David Suzuki
1930 Steve McQueen
1874 Harry Houdini

March 30
1962 M.C. Hammer
1954 The Yonge Street subway line, the first subway system in Canada, opens in Toronto
1945 Eric Clapton
1853 Vincent van Gogh

March 25
Waffle Day (Sweden)
1947 Elton John

March 31
1971 Pavel Bure
1943 Christopher Walken
1928 Gordie Howe
1596 René Descartes

April 01
All Fools' Day
Edible Book Day
1924 Royal Canadian Air
    Force is formed
1815 Otto von Bismarck

April 02
1975 Construction of the CN
    Tower is completed
1939 Marvin Gaye
1902 First full-time movie
    theater opens (Los Angeles,
    Califonia)
1875 Walter Chrysler

April 03
1961 Eddie Murphy
1958 Alec Baldwin
1942 Wayne Newton
1924 Marlon Brando

April 04
1979 Heath Ledger
1973 David Blaine
1928 Maya Angelou
1913 Muddy Waters

April 05
Cold Food Festival (China)
1916 Gregory Peck
1908 Bette Davis
1599 Thomas Hobbes

April 06
New Beer's Eve (USA)
1952 Michel Larocque
1947 John Ratzenberger
1483 Raphael

April 07
World Health Day
1964 Russell Crowe
1954 Jackie Chan
1915 Billie Holiday

April 08
Buddha's Birthday (Japan)
1968 Patricia Arquette
1963 Julian Lennon
1893 First recorded college
    basketball game
    (Pennsylvania)

April 09
Vimy Ridge Day (Canada)
1954 Dennis Quaid
1926 Hugh Hefner
1821 Charles Baudelaire

April 10
1952 Steven Seagal
1936 John Madden
1916 PGA is created
1847 Joseph Pulitzer

April 11
1970 Trevor Linden
1947 Meshach Taylor
1932 Joel Grey
1775 James Parkinson

April 12
1980 Terry Fox begins his "Marathon of Hope"
1956 Andy Garcia
1947 David Letterman
1940 Herbie Hancock

April 13
New Year festivals (South and Southeast Asia)
1951 Max Weinberg
1946 Al Green
1743 Thomas Jefferson

April 14
1977 Sarah Michelle Gellar
1945 Ritchie Blackmore
1941 Pete Rose
1932 Loretta Lynn

April 15
Jackie Robinson Day (MLB)
1982 Seth Rogen
1924 Rand McNally publishes its first road atlas
1452 Leonardo da Vinci

April 16
1965 Martin Lawrence
1947 Kareem Abdul-Jabbar
1889 Charlie Chaplin
1867 Wilbur Wright

April 17
Women's Day (Gabon)
1974 Victoria "Posh Spice" Beckham

1972 Jennifer Garner
1970 Apollo 13 spacecraft returns to Earth safely

April 18
1972 Eli Roth
1963 Conan O'Brien
1947 James Woods
1923 Yankee Stadium opens

April 19
Bicycle Day
1979 Kate Hudson
1948 Stuart McLean
1935 Dudley Moore

April 20
1972 Carmen Electra
1951 Luther Vandross
1949 Jessica Lange
1937 George Takei

April 21
1952 Secretary's Day (now Administrative Professionals' Day) is first celebrated
1951 Tony Danza
1947 Iggy Pop
1926 Queen Elizabeth II

April 22
Earth Day
1950 Peter Frampton
1923 Bettie Page
1899 Vladimir Nabokov

April 23
1936 Roy Orbison
1928 Shirley Temple
1897 Lester B. Pearson
1564 William Shakespeare

April 24
Democracy Day (Nepal)
1964 Cedric the Entertainer
1942 Barbra Streisand
1934 Shirley MacLaine

April 25
DNA Day
1969 Renee Zellweger
1940 Al Pacino
1918 Ella Fitzgerald

April 26
World Intellectual Property
    Day
1963 Jet Li
1933 Carol Burnett
1785 John James Audubon

April 27
Freedom Day (South Africa)
1959 Sheena Easton
1932 Casey Kasem
1791 Samuel Morse (Code)

April 28
1981 Jessica Alba
1974 Penelope Cruz
1950 Jay Leno
1926 Harper Lee

April 29
International Dance Day
1970 Uma Thurman
1954 Jerry Seinfeld
1899 Duke Ellington

April 30
1982 Kirsten Dunst
1959 Paul Gross
1959 Stephen Harper
1933 Willie Nelson

May 01
Lei Day (Hawaii)
1967 Tim McGraw
1954 Ray Parker, Jr.
1923 Joseph Heller

May 02
1975 David Beckam
1972 Dwayne "The Rock"
    Johnson
1955 Donatella Versace
1932 First airing of comedian
    Jack Benny's radio show

May 03
1937 Frankie Valli
1928 James Brown
1921 Sugar Ray Robinson
1903 Bing Crosby

May 04
Greenery Day (Japan)
Star Wars Day
1959 Randy Travis
1929 Audrey Hepburn

May 05
Cinco de Mayo (Mexico)
1978 First Ben & Jerry's ice
cream parlor opens
1943 Michael Palin
1818 Karl Marx

May 06
1961 George Clooney
1945 Bob Seger
1915 Orson Welles
1856 Sigmund Freud

May 07
1965 Owen Hart
1919 Eva Perón
1901 Gary Cooper
1840 Pyotr Ilich Tchaikovsky

May 08
1975 Enrique Iglesias
1944 Gary Glitter
1926 Don Rickles
1884 Harry S. Truman

May 09
1965 Steve Yzerman
1949 Billy Joel
1946 Candice Bergen
1940 James L. Brooks

May 10
1978 Kenan Thompson
1960 Bono
1957 Sid Vicious
1899 Fred Astaire

May 11
1933 Louis Farrakkan
1932 Valentino
1924 Mercedes-Benz
is formed
1904 Salvadore Dali

May 12
1968 Tony Hawk
1966 Stephen Baldwin
1962 Emilio Estevez
1937 George Carlin

May 13
1964 Stephen Colbert
1950 Stevie Wonder
1941 Ritchie Valens
1939 Harvey Keitel

May 14
1984 Mark Zuckerberg
1971 Sofia Coppola
1944 George Lucas
1796 First smallpox
vaccination is administered

May 15
1975 Ray Lewis
1948 Brian Eno
1943 David Cronenberg
1928 Mickey Mouse stars in
a cartoon

May 16
1973 Tori Spelling
1966 Janet Jackson
1919 Liberace
1866 Root beer is invented

May 17
1970 Jordan Knight
1956 Sugar Ray Leonard
1956 Bob Saget
1936 Dennis Hopper

May 18
International Museum Day
1970 Tina Fey
1955 Chow Yun-Fat
1952 George Strait

May 19
1952 Grace Jones
1951 Joey Ramone
1946 Andre the Giant
1925 Malcolm X

May 20
1972 Busta Rhymes
1946 Cher
1944 Joe Cocker
1908 Jimmy Stewart

May 21
1972 Notorious B.I.G.
1952 Mr. T
1939 Canadian National War
    Memorial is unveiled
    (Ottawa)
1917 Raymond Burr

May 22
1970 Naomi Campbell
1930 Harvey Milk
1907 Laurence Olivier
1859 Sir Arthur Conan Doyle

May 23
Labour Day (Jamaica)
World Turtle Day
1958 Drew Carey
1952 Marvin Hagler

May 24
1944 Patti LaBelle
1941 Bob Dylan
1938 Tommy Chong
1819 Queen Victoria

May 25
Africa Day (African Union)
Geek Pride Day
1975 Lauryn Hill
1963 Mike Myers

May 26
National Paper Airplane Day
    (USA)
1964 Lenny Kravitz
1926 Miles Davis
1907 John Wayne

May 27
1975 Jamie Oliver
1945 Bruce Cockburn
1911 Vincent Price
1837 Wild Bill Hickok

May 28
1979 Jesse Bradford
1968 Kylie Minogue
1945 John Fogerty
1944 Gladys Knight

May 29
1961 Melissa Etheridge
1956 LaToya Jackson
1917 John Fitzgerald Kennedy
1903 Bob Hope

May 30
Canary Islands Day (Canary
  Islands)
1964 Wynonna Judd
1909 Benny Goodman
1832 The Rideau Canal opens
  (Ottawa/eastern Ontario)

May 31
1976 Colin Farrell
1965 Brooke Shields
1930 Clint Eastwood
1819 Walt Whitman

June 01
1973 Heidi Klum
1937 Morgan Freeman
1926 Andy Griffith
1926 Marilyn Monroe

June 02
1978 Justin Long
1972 Wayne Brady
1955 Dana Carvey
1941 Charlie Watts

June 03
1989 SkyDome (now Rogers
  Centre) opens in Toronto
1967 Anderson Cooper
1942 Curtis Mayfield
1925 Tony Curtis

June 04
National Unity Day
  (Hungary)
1975 Russell Brand
1975 Angelina Jolie
1971 Noah Wyle

June 05
World Environment Day
1971 Mark Wahlberg
1956 Kenny G
1939 Joe Clark

June 06
1967 Paul Giamatti
1965 Cam Neely
1955 Sandra Bernhard
1901 Sukarno

June 07
1981 Anna Kournikova
1958 Prince
1848 Paul Gauguin
1940 Tom Jones

June 08
1977 Kayne West
1975 Bryan McCabe
1937 Joan Rivers
1867 Frank Lloyd Wright

June 09
1981 Natalie Portman
1963 Johnny Depp
1961 Michael J. Fox
1936 Jackie Mason

June 10
1965 Elizabeth Hurley
1959 Eliot Spitzer
1928 Maurice Sendak
1922 Judy Garland

June 11
1986 Shia LaBeouf
1959 Hugh Laurie
1956 Joe Montana
1910 Jacques Cousteau

June 12
Loving Day (USA)
1959 Scott Thompson
1929 Anne Frank
1924 George H.W. Bush

June 13
1986 Ashley Olsen
1986 Mary-Kate Olsen
1954 Tim Allen
1865 William Butler Yeats

June 14
1961 Boy George
1946 Donald Trump
1938 Superman's first
   appearance in a comic book
1928 Che Guevara

June 15
1973 Neil Patrick Harris
1969 Ice Cube
1964 Courteney Cox
1954 Jim Belushi
1922 Art Jones

June 16
1971 Tupac Shakur
1955 Laurie Metcalf
1943 Joan Van Ark
1890 Stan Laurel

June 17
1980 Venus Williams
1945 Art Bell
1943 Barry Manilow
1898 M.C. Escher

June 18
International Sushi Day
1952 Isabella Rossellini
1942 Roger Ebert
1942 Paul McCartney

June 19
1962 Paula Abdul
1948 Phylicia Rashad
1947 Salman Rushdie
1903 Lou Gehrig

June 20
International Surfing Day
1967 Nicole Kidman
1952 John Goodman
1949 Lionel Richie

June 21
1982 Prince William
1973 Juliette Lewis
1947 Meredith Baxter Birney
1905 Jean-Paul Sartre

June 22
1964 Dan Brown
1960 Erin Brokovich
1953 Cyndi Lauper
1949 Meryl Streep

June 23
1972 Selma Blair
1971 Felix Potvin
1957 Frances McDormand
1894 Alfred Kinsey

June 24
1947 Mick Fleetwood
1944 Jeff Beck
1895 Jack Dempsey
1604 Samuel de Champlain
    discovers present-day Saint
    John, New Brunswick

June 25
1963 George Michael
1956 Anthony Bourdain
1945 Carly Simon
1903 George Orwell

June 26
1974 Derek Jeter
1956 Chris Isaak
1892 Pearl S. Buck
1854 Sir Robert Borden

June 27
Canadian Multiculturalism
    Day
1975 Tobey Maguire
1927 Captain Kangaroo
1880 Helen Keller

June 28
1966 John Cusack
1948 Kathy Bates
1926 Mel Brooks
1491 Henry VIII

June 29
Haro Wine Festival
    (La Rioja)
1948 Fred Grandy
1947 Richard Lewis
1944 Gary Busey

June 30
1987 The Royal Canadian
    Mint introduces the loonie
1975 Ralf Schumacher
1966 Mike Tyson
1917 Lena Horne

July 01
Canada Day
1967 Pamela Anderson
1961 Princess Diana
1952 Dan Aykroyd

July 02
World UFO Day
1986 Lindsay Lohan
1957 Bret "The Hitman" Hart
1921 Sir Charles Tupper

July 03
1962 Tom Cruise
1956 Montel Williams
1883 Franz Kafka
1870 R.B. Bennett

July 04
1943 Geraldo Rivera
1927 Neil Simon
1918 Ann Landers
1847 James Anthony Bailey
    (Barnum & Baileys Circus)

July 05
1968 Nardwuar the
    Human Serviette
1950 Huey Lewis
1937 Spam (the meat) is
    first introduced
1810 P.T. Barnum

July 06
1975 50 Cent
1946 George W. Bush
1946 Sylvester Stallone
1935 The 14th Dalai Lama

July 07
Unity Factory Day (Yemen)
1949 Shelley Duvall
1940 Ringo Starr
1887 Marc Chagall

July 08
1961 Toby Keith
1958 Kevin Bacon
1951 Anjelica Huston
1949 Wolfgang Puck

July 09
1964 Courtney Love
1956 Tom Hanks
1952 John Tesh
1946 Bon Scott

July 10
1947 Arlo Guthrie
1943 Arthur Ashe
1931 Alice Munro
1856 Nikola Tesla

July 11
World Population Day
1934 Giorgio Armani
1915 Yul Brynner
1914 Babe Ruth plays his first
    major league baseball game

July 12
1951 Cheryl Ladd
1948 Richard Simmons
1937 Bill Cosby
1817 Henry David Thoreau

July 13
1946 Richard "Cheech" Marin
1942 Harrison Ford
1940 Patrick Stewart
100 BC Julius Caesar

July 14
Bastille Day (France)
1918 Ingmar Bergman
1913 Gerald R. Ford
1912 Woody Guthrie

July 15
1973 Buju Banton
1961 Forest Whittaker
1951 Jesse Ventura
1606 Rembrandt

July 16
1971 Corey Feldman
1967 Will Ferrell
1958 Michael Flatley
1907 Orville Redenbacher

July 17
1952 David Hasselhoff
1935 Donald Sutherland
1917 Phyllis Diller
1899 James Cagney

July 18
1967 Vin Diesel
1950 Richard Branson
1937 Hunter S. Thompson
1918 Nelson Mandela

July 19
1962 Anthony Edwards
1960 Atom Egoyan
1834 Edgar Degas
1814 Samuel Colt

July 20
Friend's Day
   (South America)
1980 Gisele Bundchen
1958 Billy Mays
1947 Carlos Santana

July 21
1957 Jon Lovitz
1951 Robin Williams
1911 Marshall McLuhan
1899 Ernest Hemingway

July 22
Pi Approximation Day
1954 Al Di Meola
1947 Danny Glover
1940 Alex Trebek

July 23
1989 Daniel Radcliffe
1965 Slash
1961 Woody Harrelson
1892 Haile Selassie

July 24
1969 Jennifer Lopez
1949 Michael Richards
1914 Ed Mirvish
1897 Amelia Earhart

July 25
1967 Matt Le Blanc
1957 Steve Podborsky
1954 Walter Payton
1923 Estelle Getty

July 26
1959 Kevin Spacey
1943 Mick Jagger
1928 Stanley Kubrick
1875 Carl Jung

July 27
National Sleepyhead Day
   (Finland)
1975 Alex Rodriguez
1969 Triple H
1931 Jerry Van Dyke

July 28

1948 Sally Struthers
1929 Jacqueline Kennedy
    Onassis
1887 Marcel Duchamp
1866 Beatrix Potter

July 29

1977 Danger Mouse
1953 Ken Burns
1953 Geddy Lee
1938 Peter Jennings

July 30

1974 Hilary Swank
1961 Laurence Fishburne
1947 Arnold Schwarzenegger
1863 Henry Ford

July 31

Ka Hae Hawaii Day (Hawaii)
1966 Dean Cain
1965 J.K. Rowling
1962 Wesley Snipes

August 01

World Scout Day
1981 MTV airs its first music
    video
1942 Jerry Garcia
1936 Yves St. Laurent

August 02

1970 Kevin Smith
1964 Mary-Louise Parker
1939 Wes Craven
1932 Peter O'Toole

August 03

1970 Tom Brady
1941 Martha Stewart
1940 Martin Sheen
1926 Tony Bennett

August 04

1961 Barack Obama
1955 Billy Bob Thornton
1921 Maurice Richard
1901 Louis Armstrong

August 05

International Beer Day
1946 Loni Anderson
1930 Neil Armstrong
1877 Tom Thomson

August 06

Independence Day (Jamaica)
1928 Andy Warhol
1917 Robert Mitchum
1911 Lucille Ball

August 07

1987 Sidney Crosby
1975 Charlize Theron
1960 David Duchovny
1903 Louis Leakey

August 08

Farmer's Day (Tanzania)
1961 The Edge
1947 Ken Dryden
1937 Dustin Hoffman

August 09
Frank Zappa Day (Baltimore, Maryland)
National Peacekeepers' Day (Canada)
1963 Whitney Houston
1957 Melanie Griffith

August 10
1960 Antonio Banderas
1959 Rosanna Arquette
1947 Ian Anderson
1933 Doyle Brunson

August 11
1953 Hulk Hogan
1950 Steve Wozniak
1933 Jerry Falwell
1921 Alex Haley

August 12
1971 Pete Sampras
1963 Sir Mix-a-Lot
1949 Mark Knopfler
1939 George Hamilton

August 13
International Lefthanders Day
1949 Bobby Clarke
1899 Alfred Hitchcock
1860 Annie Oakley

August 14
Independence Day (Pakistan)
1983 Mila Kunis
1966 Halle Berry
1959 Magic Johnson
1945 Steve Martin

August 15
1972 Ben Affleck
1969 Woodstock opens
1925 Oscar Peterson
1912 Julia Child

August 16
1962 Steve Carrell
1958 Angela Bassett
1958 Madonna
1954 James Cameron

August 17
1960 Sean Penn
1943 Robert De Niro
1893 Mae West
1887 Marcus Garvey

August 18
1969 Christian Slater
1957 Denis Leary
1952 Patrick Swayze
1936 Robert Redford

August 19
World Humanitarian Day
1969 Matthew Perry
1963 John Stamos
1946 Bill Clinton

August 20
1948 Robert Plant
1942 Isaac Hayes
1931 Don King
1920 The National Football League is founded

August 21
1952 Joe Strummer
1938 Kenny Rogers
1936 Wilt Chamberlain
1904 Count Basie

August 22
1973 Beenie Man
1970 Giada De Laurentis
1912 John Lee Hooker
1864 The Red Cross
   is formed

August 23
1978 Kobe Bryant
1970 River Phoenix
1949 Shelley Long
1949 Rick Springfield

August 24
1973 Dave Chappelle
1962 Craig Kilborn
1960 Cal Ripken, Jr.
1958 Stephen Fry

August 25
1954 Elvis Costello
1949 Gene Simmons
1931 Regis Philbin
1930 Sean Connery

August 26
1960 Branford Marsalis
1957 Rick Hansen
1910 Mother Teresa
1898 Peggy Guggenheim

August 27
1953 Alex Lifeson
1952 Pee-wee Herman
1908 Lyndon B. Johnson
1890 Man Ray

August 28
1969 Jack Black
1965 Shania Twain
1913 Robertson Davies
1828 Leo Tolstoy

August 29
1958 Michael Jackson
1938 Elliott Gould
1920 Charlie Parker, Jr.
1780 Jean Ingres

August 30
1982 Andy Roddick
1943 R. Crumb
1896 Raymond Massey
1797 Mary Shelley

August 31
1972 Chris Tucker
1949 Richard Gere
1945 Van Morrison
1931 Jean Beliveau

September 01
1957 Gloria Estefan
1950 Dr. Phil McGraw
1923 Rocky Marciano
1868 Henri Bourassa

September 02
1966 Salma Hayek
1965 Lennox Lewis
1964 Keanu Reeves
1959 Guy Laliberté

September 03
1965 Charlie Sheen
1913 Alan Ladd
1875 Ferdinand Porsche
1810 Paul Kane

September 04
Newspaper Carrier Day
   (USA)
1998 Google is founded
1981 Beyonce Knowles
1960 Damon Wayans

September 05
1969 Dweezil Zappa
1951 Michael Keaton
1946 Freddie Mercury
1847 Jesse James

September 06
1964 Rosie Perez
1958 Jeff Foxworthy
1957 Michaëlle Jean
1947 Jane Curtin

September 07
1949 Gloria Gaynor
1936 Buddy Holly
1914 James Van Allen
1533 Queen Elizabeth I

September 08
1979 Pink
1971 David Arquette
1932 Patsy Cline
1925 Peter Sellers

September 09
1980 Michelle Williams
1975 Michael Bublé
1966 Adam Sandler
1960 Hugh Grant

September 10
1945 José Feliciano
1933 Karl Lagerfeld
1929 Arnold Palmer
1968 Guy Ritchie

September 11
1977 Ludacris
1967 Harry Connick Jr.
1965 Moby
1961 The World Wildlife
   Fund is founded

September 12
1981 Jennifer Hudson
1980 Yao Ming
1944 Barry White
1931 George Jones

September 13
Programmers' Day
1925 Mel Tormé
1916 Roald Dahl
1775 Laura Secord

September 14
1984 Adam Lambert
1983 Amy Winehouse
1973 Nas
1960 Callum Keith Rennie

September 15
1984 Prince Harry
1946 Tommy Lee Jones
1946 Oliver Stone
1890 Agatha Christie

September 16
1956 David Copperfield
1952 Mickey Rourke
1925 B.B. King
1924 Lauren Bacall

September 17
1985 Alexander Ovechkin
1948 John Ritter
1931 Anne Bancroft
1923 Hank Williams

September 18
1971 Lance Armstrong
1961 James Gandolfini
1905 Greta Garbo
1895 John Diefenbaker

September 19
Talk Like a Pirate Day
1974 Jimmy Fallon
1960 Mario Batali
1928 Adam West

September 20
1951 Guy Lafleur
1934 Sophia Loren
1928 Dr. Joyce Brothers
1891 First gasoline-powered
      car is released

September 21
1950 Bill Murray
1947 Stephen King
1945 Jerry Bruckheimer
1866 H.G. Wells

September 22
One Web Day
1958 Andrea Bocelli
1958 Joan Jett
1791 Michael Faraday

September 23
1959 Jason Alexander
1949 Bruce Springsteen
1930 Ray Charles
1920 Mickey Rooney

September 24
1962 Nia Vardalos
1948 Phil Hartman
1936 Jim Henson
1896 F. Scott Fitzgerald

September 25
1968 Will Smith
1952 Christopher Reeve
1944 Michael Douglas
1929 Barbara Walters

September 26
1981 Serena Williams
1948 Olivia Newton-John
1914 Jack LaLanne
1888 T.S. Eliot

September 27
1984 Avril Lavigne
1972 Gwyneth Paltrow
1947 Meat Loaf
1943 Randy Bachman

September 28
1987 Hilary Duff
1967 Mira Sorvino
1901 Ed Sullivan
551 BC Confucius

September 29
Inventor's Day (Argentina)
1948 Bryant Gumbel
1935 Jerry Lee Lewis
1901 Enrico Fermi

September 30
1971 Jenna Elfman
1957 Fran Drescher
1924 Truman Capote
1882 Hans Geiger

October 01
World Vegetarian Day
1935 Julie Andrews
1924 Jimmy Carter
1920 Walter Matthau

October 02
1951 Sting
1950 Charles M. Schulz's
    "Peanuts" is first published
1890 Groucho Marx
1869 Mahatma Gandhi

October 03
1969 Gwen Stefani
1954 Stevie Ray Vaughan
1941 Chubby Checker
1882 A.Y. Jackson

October 04
Cinnamon Roll Day (Sweden)
1976 Alicia Silverstone
1946 Susan Sarandon
1923 Charlton Heston

October 05
1965 Mario Lemieux
1965 Patrick Roy
1957 Bernie Mac
1951 Bob Geldof

October 06
1970 Amy Jo Johnson
1963 Elisabeth Shue
1889 Thomas Edison shows
    his first motion picture
1744 James McGill

October 07
1968 Toni Braxton
1955 Yo-Yo Ma
1951 John Mellencamp
1931 Desmond Tutu

October 08
1970 Matt Damon
1949 Sigourney Weaver
1943 Chevy Chase
1941 Rev. Jesse Jackson

October 09
World Post Day
1952 Sharon Osbourne
1948 Jackson Browne
1940 John Lennon

October 10
1974 Dale Earnhardt, Jr.
1969 Brett Favre
1954 David Lee Roth
1917 Thelonious Monk

October 11
Old Michelmas Day (Celtic)
1965 Luke Perry
1962 Joan Cusack
1844 Henry Heinz

October 12
1970 Kirk Cameron
1968 Hugh Jackman
1935 Luciano Pavarotti
1810 First Oktoberfest

October 13
1971 Sacha Baron Cohen
1959 Marie Osmond
1947 Sammy Hagar
1941 Paul Simon

October 14
1978 Usher
1939 Ralph Lauren
1927 Roger Moore
1894 e.e. cummings

October 15
1959 Sarah Ferguson
1959 Emeril Lagasse
1926 Michel Foucault
1844 Friedrich Nietzsche

October 16
Boss's Day
    (USA and Canada)
1946 Suzanne Somers
1925 Angela Lansbury
1854 Oscar Wilde

October 17
1972 Eminem
1969 Wyclef Jean
1963 Norm MacDonald
1938 Evel Knievel

October 18
1961 Wynton Marsalis
1960 Jean Claude Van
    Damme
1926 Chuck Berry
1919 Pierre Trudeau

October 19
1962 Evander Holyfield
1945 John Lithgow
1944 Peter Tosh
1931 John le Carré

October 20
1971 Snoop Dogg
1950 Tom Petty
1931 Mickey Mantle
1882 Bela Lugosi

October 21
1956 Carrie Fisher
1942 Judge Judy Sheindlin
1917 Dizzy Gillespie
1833 Alfred Nobel

October 22
1968 Shaggy
1952 Jeff Goldblum
1946 Deepak Chopra
1938 Christopher Lloyd

October 23
1959 "Weird" Al Yankovic
1957 Martin Luther King III
1942 Michael Chichton
1925 Johnny Carson

October 24
United Nations Day
1947 Kevin Kline
1936 Bill Wyman
1901 Annie Edson Taylor goes
   over Niagara Falls in a barrel
   (the first person to do so)

October 25
1972 Jonathan Torrens
1928 Marion Ross
1881 Pablo Picasso
1861 The Toronto Stock
   Exchange is created

October 26
1977 Jon Heder
1967 Keith Urban
1962 Cary Elwes
1946 Pat Sajak

October 27
1939 John Cleese
1932 Sylvia Plath
1928 Gilles Vigneault
1858 Theodore Roosevelt

October 28
International Animation Day
1955 Bill Gates
1937 Charlie Daniels
1914 Dr. Jonas Salk

October 29
1971 Winona Ryder
1957 Dan Castellaneta
1953 Denis Potvin
1947 Richard Dreyfuss

October 30
Mischief Night (USA)
1939 Grace Slick
1821 Fyodor Dostoevsky
1735 John Adams

October 31
Halloween
1967 Vanilla Ice
1963 Rob Schneider
1950 John Candy

November 01
World Vegan Day
1959 Jacques Plante, goalie for the Montreal Canadiens, is the first player to wear a protective mask in an NHL game
1957 Lyle Lovett
1942 Larry Flynt

November 02
All Souls Day
1966 David Schwimmer
1961 k.d. lang
1936 The Canadian Broadcasting Corporation is established

November 03
1957 Dolph Lundgren
1953 Dennis Miller
1952 Roseanne Barr
1817 Bank of Montreal, Canada's oldest chartered bank, opens

November 04
Day of Love (Egypt)
1969 Sean "P. Diddy" Combs
1969 Matthew McConaughey
1960 Kathy Griffin

November 05
Guy Fawkes Night
1960 Tilda Swinton
1959 Bryan Adams
1941 Art Garfunkel

November 06
1972 Thandie Newton
1972 Rebecca Romijn
1970 Ethan Hawke
1946 Sally Field

November 07
1943 Joni Mitchell
1918 Billy Graham
1913 Albert Camus
1867 Marie Curie

November 08
1966 Gordon Ramsay
1949 Bonnie Raitt
1847 Bram Stoker
1656 Edmund Halley

November 09
Inventor's Day (Germany, Australia, Switzerland)
1970 Chris Jericho
1951 Lou Ferrigno
1934 Carl Sagan

November 10
1977 Brittany Murphy
1968 Tracy Morgan
1956 Sinbad
1484 Martin Luther

November 11
Singles Day (China)
1974 Leonardo DiCaprio
1962 Demi Moore
1922 Kurt Vonnegut, Jr.

November 12
1982 Anne Hathaway
1980 Ryan Gosling
1945 Neil Young
1929 Grace Kelly

November 13
World Kindness Day
1967 Jimmy Kimmel
1955 Whoopi Goldberg
1850 Robert Louis Stevenson

November 14
1954 Yanni
1948 Prince Charles
1891 Frederick Banting
1840 Claude Monet

November 15
1957 Kevin Eubanks
1940 Sam Waterston
1932 Petula Clark
1929 Ed Asner

November 16
1977 Oksana Baiul
1967 Lisa Bonet
1966 Dean McDermott
19?? Shawn Mulligan

November 17
1978 Rachel McAdams
1944 Danny DeVito
1942 Martin Scorsese
1938 Gordon Lightfoot

November 18
1974 Chloë Sevigny
1953 Kevin Nealon
1923 Alan Shepard

1883 Five standard time
zones are instituted in
North America

November 19
World Toilet Day
1962 Jodie Foster
1961 Meg Ryan
1942 Calvin Klein

November 20
Universal Children's Day
1947 Joe Walsh
1889 Edwin Hubble
1841 Sir Wilfrid Laurier

November 21
World Hello Day
1965 Bjork
1945 Goldie Hawn
1694 Voltaire

November 22
1984 Scarlett Johansson
1967 Mark Ruffalo
1958 Jamie Lee Curtis
1940 Terry Gilliam

November 23
1992 Miley Cyrus
1888 Harpo Marx
1887 Boris Karloff
1859 Billy The Kid

November 24
Evolution Day
1978 Katherine Heigl
1867 Scott Joplin
1864 Henri de
Toulouse-Lautrec

November 25
1971 Christina Applegate
1960 John F. Kennedy, Jr.
1944 Ben Stein
1914 Joe DiMaggio

November 26
1939 Tina Turner
1927 Ernie Coombs
  (Mr. Dressup)
1922 Charles Schulz
1917 The National Hockey
  League is formed

November 27
1976 Jaleel White
1955 Bill Nye
1942 Jimi Hendrix
1940 Bruce Lee

November 28
1967 Anna Nicole Smith
1962 Jon Stewart
1950 Ed Harris
1943 Randy Newman

November 29
1964 Don Cheadle
1955 Howie Mandel
1949 Garry Shandling
1898 C.S. Lewis
1832 Louisa May Alcott

November 30
1965 Ben Stiller
1955 Billy Idol
1937 Ridley Scott
1835 Mark Twain

December 01
1945 Bette Midler
1940 Richard Pryor

1935 Woody Allen
1935 Lou Rawls

December 02
1981 Britney Spears
1978 Nelly Furtado
1968 Lucy Liu
1946 Gianni Versace

December 03
1968 Brendan Fraser
1960 Darryl Hannah
1960 Julianne Moore
1948 Ozzy Osbourne

December 04
1973 Tyra Banks
1969 Jay-Z
1949 Jeff Bridges
1909 The first Grey Cup game
  is played

December 05
1968 Margaret Cho
1933 Prohibition ends in
  the USA
1932 Little Richard
1901 Walt Disney

December 06
Saint Nicholas Day
1956 Randy Rhoads
1955 Steven Wright
1920 Dave Brubeck

December 07
International Civil Aviation Day
1956 Larry Bird
1949 Tom Waits
1928 Noam Chomsky

December 08
1966 Sinéad O'Connor
1953 Kim Basinger
1943 Jim Morrison
1925 Sammy Davis, Jr.

December 09
1962 Felicity Huffman
1957 Donny Osmond
1953 John Malkovich
1916 Kirk Douglas

December 10
Human Rights Day
    (International)
1985 Raven-Symone
1964 Bobby Flay
1960 Kenneth Branagh

December 11
Tango Day (Buenos Aires)
1973 Mos Def
1954 Jermaine Jackson
1946 UNICEF is established

December 12
1970 Jennifer Connelly
1940 Dionne Warwick
1923 Bob Barker
1915 Frank Sinatra

December 13
1967 Jamie Foxx
1957 Steve Buscemi
1948 Ted Nugent
1925 Dick Van Dyke

December 14
1988 Vanessa Hudgens
1951 Paul "Beakman" Zaloom
1947 NASCAR is founded
1503 Nostradamus

December 15
1979 Adam Brody
1949 Don Johnson
1832 Gustave Eiffel
37 Nero

December 16
1967 Donovan Bailey
1917 Arthur C. Clarke
1775 Jane Austen
1770 Ludwig van Beethoven

December 17
1975 Milla Jovovich
1953 Bill Pullman
1946 Eugene Levy
1874 W.L. Mackenzie King

December 18
1980 Christina Aguilera
1963 Brad Pitt
1946 Steven Spielberg
1943 Keith Richards

December 19
1972 Alyssa Milano
1970 Tyson Beckford
1961 Reggie White
1915 Edith Piaf

December 20
1983 Jonah Hill
1957 Billy Bragg
1946 Uri Geller
1868 Harvey Firestone

December 21
1966 Keifer Sutherland
1948 Samuel L. Jackson
1940 Frank Zappa
1937 Jane Fonda

December 22
Dongzhi Festival (East Asia)
1962 Ralph Fiennes
1945 Diane Sawyer
1938 Lucien Bouchard

December 23
Festivus
1964 Eddie Vedder
1943 Harry Shearer
1929 Chet Baker

December 24
Christmas Eve
1945 Steve Smith
   (Red Green)
1922 Ava Gardner
1905 Howard Hughes

December 25
Christmas Day
1946 Jimmy Buffett
1899 Humphrey Bogart
1642 Sir Isaac Newton

December 26
Boxing Day
First day of Kwanzaa
1971 Jared Leto
1921 Steve Allen

December 27
1970 Chyna
1966 Bill Goldberg
1948 Gérard Depardieu
1822 Louis Pasteur

December 28
1981 Sienna Miller
1978 John Legend
1954 Denzel Washington
1763 John Molson

December 29
1972 Jude Law
1947 Ted Danson
1938 John Voight
1936 Mary Tyler Moore

December 30
1975 Tiger Woods
1959 Tracey Ullman
1928 Bo Diddley
1865 Rudyard Kipling

December 31
New Year's/Hangover Eve
1959 Val Kilmer
1948 Donna Summer
1943 Ben Kingsley

INTERNET LINKS

The Internet is the ultimate reference tool. Spend an hour in cyberspace before your next outing, learning the difference between Irish, Scotch and Canadian whiskey. Then perform some real-world taste tests. Impress the bartender with your vast knowledge. Astound your date!

Let me know of any interesting websites you've found by e-mailing me at *shawnmulligan@hotmail.com*. Your questions or comments about *Mulligan's* are also welcome. Cheers!

Alcohol (Ethanol)
www.encyclopedia.com/articles/04238.html
www.scifun.chem.wisc.edu/chemweek/PDF/ethanol.pdf

Bartending
cocktails.about.com
This commercial site is littered with advertisements; however, they are subtle and don't interfere with the surfing experience. Many excellent links and great content.

tor.klippan.se/~fredrik/guide/
Billed as the "(Un)official Internet Bartender's Guide," this huge database contains a cornucopia of basic and obscure recipes. I especially recommend the section on making your own liqueurs.

www.barkeep.net/
A simple site with a good shooter section (which is much like the section in the last edition of *Mulligan's*!)

www.barmedia.com
A commercial site with some interesting articles and trivia challenges.

www.barnonedrinks.com
A complete database with a good collection of drinking games.

www.bartending.com
A useful commercial site offering several recipes.

www.cocktail.com
Some interesting cocktail-related articles, but far too much advertising.

www.drinkmixer.com
A great-looking page with little, but interesting, content.

www.epact.se/acats
Plenty of recipes and a collection of the worst pick-up lines.

www.hotwired.com/cocktail
This site offers in-depth historical information on popular cocktails such as the Bloody Caesar, Bellini and martini. A must for any serious bartender.

www.idrink.com/home.htm
Over 5000 recipes are offered, but you must search for them by name.

www.mixdrinks.com
An excellent site with thousands of recipes, including shooters. Highly recommended.

www.nightclub.com
A commercial magazine offering select online articles of interest to bartenders.

www.thevirtualbar.com
The Virtual Bar answers "virtually" any question you might have about bartending. Highly recommended.

www.webtender.com
A colossus of beverage information with nearly 5000 recipes. Recommended.

Brandy
le-cognac.com/entree2_eng.html
A great tutorial on cognac.

www.charlesnealselections.com/armagnac.html
All about Armagnac.

www.courvoisier.com
www.hennessy-cognac.com

www.remy.com
The Remy Martin homepage.

www.sallys-place.com/beverages/spirits/brandy.htm
A good discussion on brandy.

Gin
www.beefeater.com
www.bombaysaphire.com
www.plymouthgin.com
www.tanqueray.com

Liqueurs
www.baileys.com
www.campari.com/oh.htm
www.chartreuse.fr
www.cointreau.com
www.grand-marnier.com
www.jagermeister.com
www.kahlua.com

www.luxardo.it
Makers of sambuca.

www.mariebrizard.com
www.micro.magnet.fsu.edu/cocktails/pages/Amaretto.html
See Amaretto under a microscope!

www.northcoast.com/~alden/Liqueurs.html
Excellent list of liqueur substitutes.

www.pernod-ricard.fr
www.schlager.com/home2.cgi
The Goldschläger homepage.

www.southerncomfort.com

Miscellaneous
www.angostura.com
www.sake.com
www.seagram.com
www.tabasco.com

Rum
www.appletonstate.com
www.bacardi.com
www.barbancourt.com
www.captainmorgan.com
www.malibu-rum.com

Sake
www.sake.com
The name says it all.

Scotch
www.chivas.com
www.glenfiddich.com
www.theglenlivet.com/home.html
www.glenmorangie.com
www.jbscotch.com/noshockfrm.htm
www.laphroaig.com

Software
www.allstats.com/bar
www.barback.com
www.probartender.com

Tequila
www.casanoble.com.mx/index2.html
www.cuervo.com

www.georgian.net/rally/tequila/links.html
This site offers links to every tequila site in the universe!!!

www.tequila.net
www.patronspirits.com

Vodka

www.absolut.com

www.absolutad.org
Absolut vodka advertisements.

www.finlandia.com
www.greygoose.com
www.iceberg.com
www.infernovodka.com
www.kryshtal.com
www.lubelska.com
www.skyy.com
www.smirnoff.com
www.stoli.com

Whiskey

www.bushmills.com
www.canadianmist.com/default.htm
www.jackdaniels.com
www.jimbeam.com

www.smallbatch.com
Knob Creek Bourbon.

MULLIGAN'S FINAL WORDS ON HANGOVERS

The word "intoxication" is derived from the Greek *toxicon*, meaning "arrow poison." Those of us who have experienced the aftereffects of intoxication know how wicked the poison can be. I give you my moral and physical antivenin, in a step-by-step fashion.

STEP 1: Sleep as long as possible. You have no good reason to be conscious.

STEP 2: Upon awakening, survey your surroundings. Greet all parties in your immediate vicinity in a friendly but cautious manner, accepting that your relation to them may be unclear at this point.

STEP 3: Remain in the fetal position while performing a quick body examination, specifically checking for new tattoos, body piercing or injuries requiring immediate medical attention.

STEP 4: Devise a cunning excuse for missing work, school or an important appointment. Dental emergencies are always a good choice, as they can be supported by the immediate, though disgusting, display of recent, "actual" dental work.

STEP 5: Re-establish balance and attempt bipedal motion. This process may require several attempts, but real progress requires mobility.

STEP 6: Unplug all telephone equipment. Resist the urge to play unheard answering machine messages, as they are probably demands for apologies or mocking reminders of your silly and/or obnoxious behavior. Avoid confrontation.

STEP 7: Begin a fluid-replacement program. Resist the urge to have a morning-after drink, as this will only lead to the catastrophic, night-after-the-morning-after hangover. Progress to solid foods when possible. Avoid confrontation.

STEP 8: Assess financial consequences of the previous night's misbehavior. Arrange Sunday dinner at parents' house to discuss financial restructuring. One plan: Claim that tuition fee increases and unforeseen lab fees have led to an immediate cash shortage.

STEP 9: Recite, repeatedly, the obligatory phrase: "I will never drink again." Although this proclamation is a sham, saying it is mandatory.

STEP 10: Return to bed, recalling Dickens' last words in *A Tale of Two Cities*: "It is a far, far better rest that I go to than I have ever known."

A crossword puzzle grid with the following filled entries:

COKE · TEQUILA · ALE · GIN · COINTREAU · KAHLUA · LIQUEUR · RUM · RYE · GRENADINE · VODKA · NISEITTA · ALIZE · OLIVE · VVD · SODA · ETHYL · VERMOUTH · BRUT · TKIR · BEER · NEAT · STOUT · TRIP · XO · PLAYERS

Crossword #2

C	H	A	M	B	O	R	D		J	O	E	
A				R						L		
F			R	O	Y		W	O	O	D	Y	
E		D	■	W					U			A
	P	E	R	N	O	D			Z			M
	A							L	O	T	T	O
	R				N			U		A		U
	F	L	A	N	A	G	A	N		B		R
	A		L		V			C				
	I		A		E		C	H	E	R	R	Y
	T		B		L		A			U		E
			A				R			S		A
C	O	S	M	O			L			T		S
H			A		S	H	A	N	D	Y		T
I		K				O						
N		I				P	U	N	C	H		
A		R	O	S	E	S						

	N	U	T	M	E	G			V	S	O	P
			A		G						U	
	D		X		G	I	B	S	O	N		
T	R	A	I	N		T		C		C	E	
	A					A		O		E		
	M					L		T				
	B	R	A	N	D	Y		C	O	R	N	
	U		M		E			H		O		
C	I	G	A	R						C		
	E		R		B		S	H	A	K	E	N
	M	E	T	A	X	A			S			
			T		I		M		O			
S	A	L	T		L		B	A	R		W	
T			O		E		U		G		I	
R					Y		C		E		N	
A	K	E			S		A	G	A	V	E	
W									T			

135